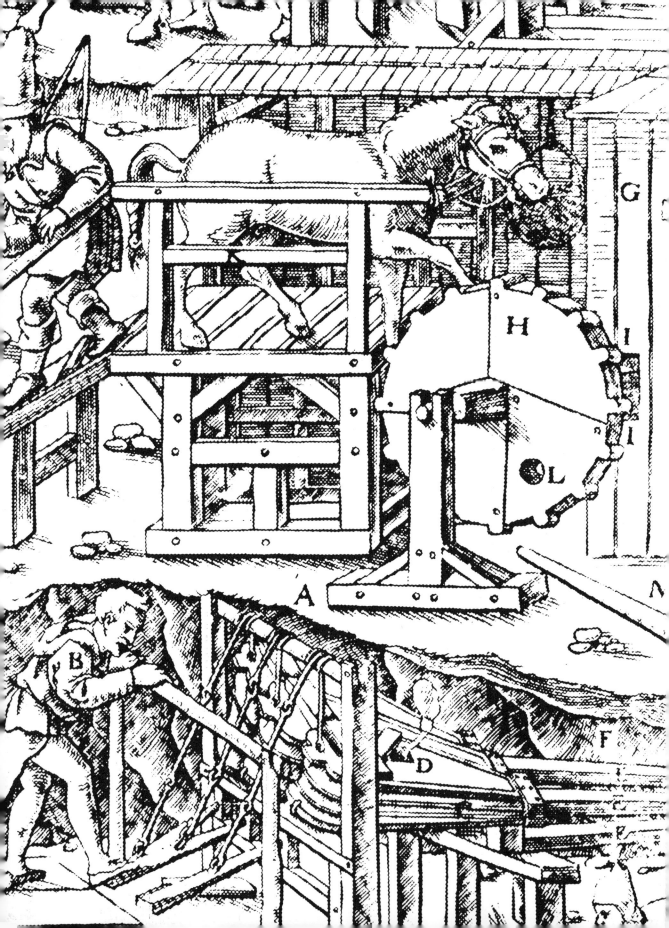

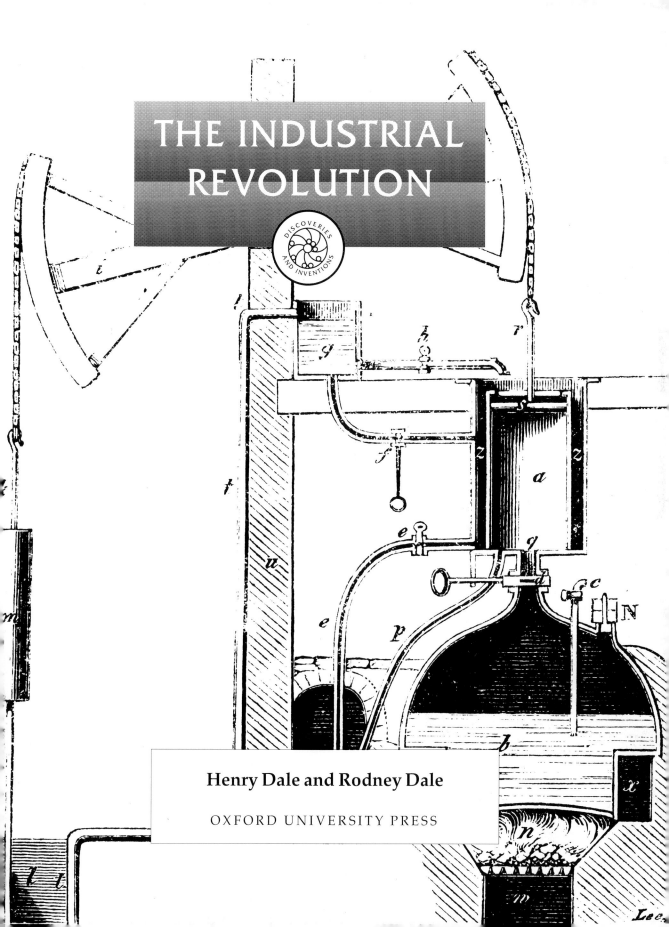

THE INDUSTRIAL REVOLUTION

Henry Dale and Rodney Dale

OXFORD UNIVERSITY PRESS

Photographic acknowledgments

All illustrations in this book have been taken from
out-of-copyright material held in the British Library's
collections, with the exception of those which carry a credit
line in the accompanying caption. Patents are numbered and
dated for ease of reference.

OXFORD UNIVERSITY PRESS

Oxford New York Toronto
Delhi Bombay Calcutta Madras Karachi
Kuala Lumpur Singapore Hong Kong Tokyo
Nairobi Dar es Salaam Cape Town
Melbourne Auckland Madrid
and associated companies in
Berlin Ibadan

Library of Congress Cataloging in Publication Data

Dale, Henry.
  The Industrial Revolution / Henry Dale, Rodney Dale.
    p.64, 24.6 x 18.9 cm. — (Discoveries and inventions)
  Includes bibliographical references (p.63) and index.
  Summary: Examines the industrial revolution, discussing
how developments in the harnessing of power and methods
of transportation changed the way we work and play.
  ISBN 0-19-520967-2 (acid-free paper)
  1. Industry—History—Juvenile literature. [1.
Industry—History.] I. Dale, Rodney, 1933- . II. Title.
III. Series.
HD2321.D35 1992
338.09′034—dc20   92-21663
                                                CIP
                                                AC

ISBN 0-19-520971 -0 (paperback)
ISBN 0-19-520967-2 (hardback)
Printing (last digit) 9 8 7 6 5 4 3 2 1

Designed and set on Ventura in Palatino by Roger Davies
Printed in Singapore

Front cover
Pit-head of a coal mine with steam winding gear *c*1820 by
an unknown artist (Walker Art Gallery, Liverpool). In spite
of the technical difficulties, some Newcomen engines were
converted to provide rotary motion (as shown). They were
cheap to build, but clumsy and coal-hungry. However, they
served well where coal was cheap – at the pit-head. In the
Midlands, they were known as 'Whimseys'.

Facing page 1
Mine-ventilation machinery – horse and man-power.

Page 1
Newcomen's steam engine – the cylinder is mounted
directly over the boiler, and the valves are operated by
hand.

Pages 2 and 3
Thomas Telford's bridge over the Menai Straits, with
details of construction.

Facing page 64
Sixteenth-century diagram of a fanciful steam turbine
operating pestles and mortars via reduction gearing.

Contents

Introduction 4

Power 6

Iron and steel 17

Mining 24

Transport 26

Textile machinery 48

Industrial chemistry 55

Agriculture 57

Chronology 63

Further Reading 63

Introduction

Power and transport

This book concentrates on two interdependent themes: power and transport.

The search for ways to generate – and use – power has moulded our development since the earliest times. First human, then animal, power was used to move and lift objects, and machines were developed such as the capstan, winch and crane. The importance of irrigation spurred the development of many ingenious systems for lifting and directing water. And the power of water itself was exploited for grinding corn and blowing furnaces. Wind, too, was harnessed – first for driving sailing vessels; later for grinding corn and pumping water. By the end of the 17th century most hand tools and components existed in a form we would recognize today. And it was about that time that the foundations of that great upsurge of activity known as the Industrial Revolution began, with radical changes in the way power was generated and exploited.

As the 18th century dawned, the power of steam was discovered and developed, to play an increasingly important part in the invention and development of a wide range of machines and processes, many of which stimulated advances in fields other than their own.

The new power changed the face of the countryside and the distribution of its growing population. Machines that could do the work of many people, and power sources that could drive many such machines, initiated a move from small-scale domestic production to factory systems employing many people in one place. Large industrial towns grew in areas providing the raw materials to fuel that growth. But, though this seems like an inevitable and logical progression, it took well over a century and was not, of course, moving purposefully towards some pre-ordained conclusion.

The development and concentration of industry demanded better transport; conversely, better transport fostered the development of industry. Once, most activities had been local, with communities producing most of what they needed themselves. With the growth of centres of activity, improved transport was needed to move raw materials in for processing, and finished goods away to the markets.

Connections

Many interconnected circumstances helped to drive the revolution. Wood became scarce, for it had been used in vast quantities to heat homes, and to turn into charcoal to smelt iron. Shortage of fuel generally, and the discovery that iron could be successfully smelted using coke, increased the demand for coal; steam engines were brought in to drain the mines for deeper working, and to provide compressed air for the blast furnaces; it was thus possible to produce increasing quantities of high-quality iron from which new machines were built. New tools and techniques gave rise to better machines, which then produced better tools – and so on.

But behind all this growth and development was the ingenuity of individual people – people with ideas, with business and managerial skills, with drive; they made it happen. For whatever reasons – a need to satisfy their curiosity, to show how clever they were, to make money – the industrial climate stimulated people to invent things, to develop them, to manufacture them and to sell them.

And what underpinned the whole process was the exploitation of coal. Coal provided steam power for the factories – and for the transport system which bound them and their markets together – as well as direct heating for iron furnaces, and gas which at first was used for lighting, and then later as an easily transportable energy source. Coal was the key to industrialization, not just of Britain, but of the whole developing world.

An early example of automatic control – Lee's windmill patent (No. 615 of 1745). When the force of the wind on the main sails is maximum, that on the fantail is zero. If the wind veers, the fantail turns, rotating the cap of the mill which carries the sails, turning them full into the wind again (at which point the fantail stops). There is also a mechanism for opening and shutting the louvres on the sails to regulate the speed.

Why 'Industrial Revolution'?

It is worth noting that the term 'Industrial Revolution' was not coined until long after what we now think of as the event. True, the words had been coupled by John Stuart Mill in 1848 ('The opening of foreign trade . . . sometimes works a complete industrial revolution in a country whose resources were completely undeveloped') but they do not appear to have been used in our context until 1884, and then as a title by Arnold Toynbee: 'Lectures on the Industrial Revolution in England'. Clearly, the word 'revolution' is used in a new way: it is not akin to the French Revolution, not a revolution against anything – it is primarily a rapid change.

5

Power

I sell sir, what all the world desires – power.
M BOULTON (1728–1809)

At the beginning of the 18th century there were three principal sources of power: wind, water, and animal (including human). But all three had drawbacks. Windmills needed sites where there was a reasonable chance of the wind blowing, but even then it could not be guaranteed. Water power was available only where there was a flow of water, and was unreliable especially in the summer when rivers and streams tended to dry up. Moreover, works built upstream could starve the supply for those lower down – the cause of many a dispute. Animal power was expensive – large powerful animals had to be fed and maintained, and their output wasn't very great. Furthermore they could not be driven indefinitely and had to be watered and rested.

At the end of the 17th century flooding in mines of all kinds – coal, tin, copper – posed a major problem. Shallow deposits had been worked out but there were rich pickings below the water table – if only they could be got out. Unfortunately, the only way of driving pumps in those days was by animal power and this was insufficient to uncover the vast reserves that waited.

In the United States, water-powered grist mills, saw-mills and textile mills were integral parts of the community from the earliest times. There was no lack of ingenuity in a people whose mission was to open and exploit that vast land and, by the end of the 18th century, America was as advanced as any other country in harnessing water power. The experience of building

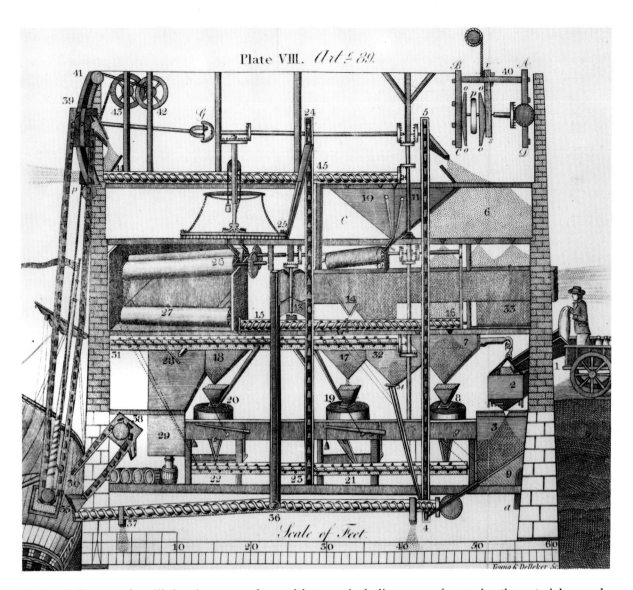

Plate VIII. *Art. 89.*

Sectional diagram of a mill showing many advanced features, including screws for moving the material around.

Left
Animal power – oxen on a sloping treadwheel driving a mill.

7

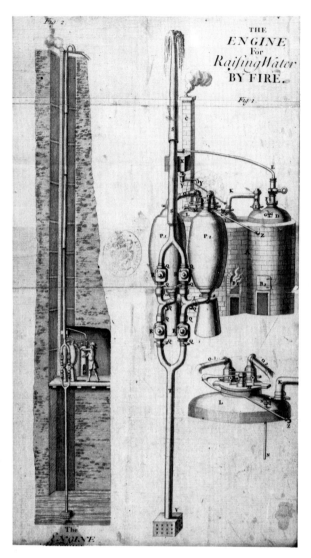

In Savery's 'Engine for Raising Water by Fire' steam from the boiler on the right is admitted alternately to the two egg-shaped vessels. When one of the vessels is full of steam, the steam is condensed, and the reduced pressure draws water from the mine through a one-way valve. The down-pipe valve is then closed, the up-pipe valve opened, and steam admitted to force the water up to the surface. Because nature decrees that even a perfect vacuum will support only 34 feet (10.4 m) of water, the height of the engine above the water level is limited. The engine is therefore built in to a niche in the mineshaft, as shown in the drawing on the left.

and running water mills was to stand the people in good stead as the powerful manufacturing nation emerged from the pioneering agricultural economy.

The Miner's Friend

Thomas Savery (?1650–1715), a military engineer, was the first person to construct a practical steam-powered water pump. Brought up near a mining district, he had long been interested in the problem of draining mines. In 1698, his patent (No 356) described his idea as a 'New invention of raiseing of water and occasioning motion to all sorts of mill work by the impellant force of fire'. In 1702 he published a description of it in a book: *The Miner's Friend*. The pump was not a steam-engine in the modern sense, but raised water by condensing steam in a vessel, creating a partial vacuum which drew the water up into it through a one-way valve. More steam was then admitted to the vessel, which pushed the water up through another valve.

Savery demonstrated a working model of his device in 1699, and in the early 1700s showed a full-size version in London. For a short while his 'engines' were used to supply water for large buildings, and to provide power indirectly by raising water for water wheels, which in turn drove other machinery. However, the valves of these engines were operated by hand, which is a much less efficient method than the engine working its own valves – doubtless, the engine used much more coal than its operators cared to pay for. Moreover, condensing steam would not lift water more than 34 feet (10.4 m) – or so the laws of physics decree – and an early picture (*left*) shows the Miner's Friend tucked into a niche hewn into the mineshaft. No wonder Savery's pumps soon fell into disuse.

The 'fire engine'

Although others tried to improve Savery's pump, the next step in the development of steam power was taken by Thomas Newcomen (1663–1729), who has been described variously as a tool dealer, ironmonger and blacksmith. Whatever his trade, Newcomen often visited mines, and realized how expensive it was to drain them by means of horse power. Unaware of Savery's patent, Newcomen, along with John Calley, set out to build a machine to pump water from mines. He spent years developing his idea only to find that

Newcomen's engine was the first successful
fire-driven machine. The engine consists of a large
boiler, and a piston within a cylinder connected to a
beam whose other end drives the pump rod. The
engine works by admitting steam at atmospheric
pressure into the cylinder whose top is closed by the
piston, whereupon the piston rises – mainly from the
weight of the pump rod at the other end of the beam.
Once the piston has reached the top of its travel, a jet
of cold water is sprayed into the cylinder and the
steam condenses, thereby reducing the pressure
below the piston. The piston is forced down by the
atmospheric pressure on its upper surface and, at its
lowest limit, the cycle starts again.

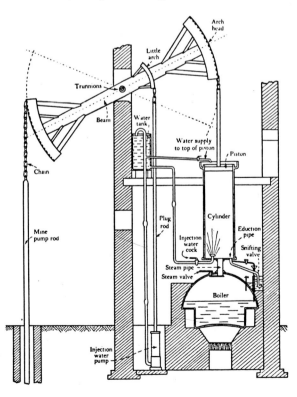

Savery held a patent covering the use of the impellant
force of fire. Newcomen therefore entered into a partnership agreement with Savery and erected his first
engine at the Dudley Castle mine in 1712.

Legend has it that Humphrey Potter, a boy employed to operate the steam and spray valves, worked
out how the engine could be made to work automat-
ically if appropriate parts of the moving machinery
were connected. It is more likely that Newcomen included automatic valve operation on his original in-
stallation; Humphrey Potter's ingenuity is a fine
example of selflessness – for would he not have done
himself out of a job? The story may have arisen from
the early use of a float or 'buoy' to open the injection
cock.

Newcomen's pump worked reasonably well and
certainly steadily, and mine owners saved much
trouble and money by installing one to replace their
working animals. Although it was inefficient compared with the best possible use of steam, a Newcomen
pumping engine pumping a mine near Whitehaven in
1750 was reported to have replaced 110 horses, or 2,520
men carrying buckets.

When Savery died in 1715, his patent rights were
acquired by an entrepreneurial group who advertised
and erected Newcomen engines all over England and
Europe, and made money from the idea until the patent expired in 1733; Newcomen died in 1729, probably
not having had much financial benefit from his own
invention.

Newcomen's engine had a profound effect on the
coal-mining industry. It provided power to pump
water from the deepest mines and opened up seams
that had previously been unworkable because of
flooding. It also created a new market for coal as growing numbers of fuel-hungry engines began to appear.
Even so, it still wasn't obvious that steam power was
the way forward for all needs. This is demonstrated by
the fact that the engineer John Smeaton conducted efficiency tests on windmills and waterwheels, and
presented the results to the Royal Society in 1759. *An
Experimental Enquiry concerning the Natural Powers of
Wind and Water to turn Mills* won him a gold medal.

In the mid-18th century there were many Newcomen engines providing power by pumping water
up to reservoirs for driving water wheels. The steam
engine could not yet provide rotary motion, because

18th-century engineering was by no means all hit and miss. This picture of what we now call a 'test rig' shows how John Smeaton addressed the 'Experimental Enquiry concerning the Natural Powers of Wind and Water to turn Mills'. The windmill is turned by pulling the cord, which swings it round on the end of the arm, thus creating its own wind.

John Smeaton (1724–92).

James Watt (1736–1819).

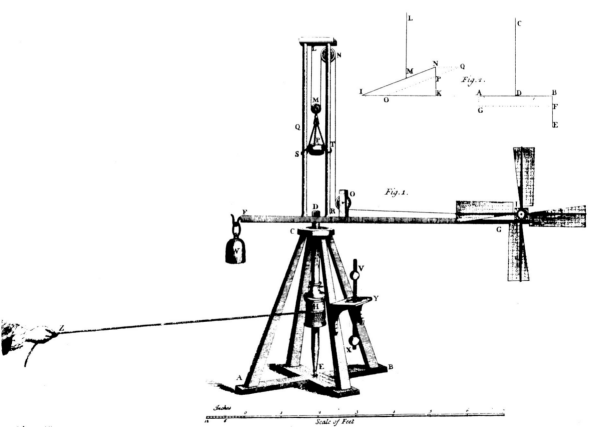

the power was transmitted via flexible links which could be pulled but not pushed.

The rotative engine

As a boy, James Watt (1736–1819) showed keen interest in geometry and in model making, so it was reasonable that at the age of 18 he should move to London to serve an apprenticeship as a mathematical instrument maker. However, his health was poor and the London air did not agree with his constitution; within a year he returned to Scotland. In about 1756 he was prevented from opening a mathematical instrument maker's shop in Glasgow by the Corporation of Hammermen, on the grounds that he had not completed his apprenticeship; fortunately, Glasgow University recognized his potential and appointed him as its mathematical instrument maker. Watt continued to improve his skills, and developed friendships with many of the University's eminent men. One such friendship – with the professor of chemistry Dr Joseph Black (1728–1799) – was to have important consequences not only for Watt, but for the Industrial Revolution.

In 1764 Watt was asked to repair a model Newcomen engine that refused to work properly despite the attentions of London's celebrated mathematical instrument maker, Jonathan Sisson (?1694–1749). Watt found it to be so inefficient that it would operate only for a few strokes before running out of steam. Watt spent some time pondering the problem before realizing that condensing the steam in the cylinder was wasteful; the cylinder had a comparatively large surface area for its volume, and rapidly cooled each time the cold-water spray condensed the steam. When a fresh charge of steam was admitted to the cylinder, 80 per cent of its energy was expended in heating the cold metal before it could do any other work, and the small boiler was not capable of supplying steam at the rate needed.

The same inefficiency occurred in full-size versions, but was less noticeable because of the smaller ratio of surface area to volume. Watt's solution, arrived at after much thought, was to keep the cylinder hot by insulating it and to provide a separate condenser connected to the cylinder by a pipe. Watt conducted such experiments on his improvement to the steam engine as his meagre funds would allow. It was then that his friendship with Joseph Black took its fortuitous twist: an

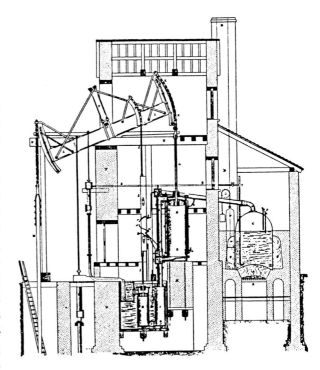

The first Watt engines (1788) were single acting in that steam is admitted to one side of the piston only.

acquaintance of Black's, Dr John Roebuck (1718–1794), owned the lease of a large coal mine in Linlithgowshire, which was proving impossible to drain with a Newcomen pump. Black told Roebuck of Watt's improved steam engine design, and Roebuck contacted Watt.

With Roebuck's financial help, Watt built an experimental engine at Roebuck's home. As moves towards improved efficiency, he tried to maintain cylinder temperature by means of a separate condenser, using a steam jacket to keep the cylinder hot, and using steam (at atmospheric pressure) instead of air to push the piston down. In 1769 Watt patented a new method of lessening the consumption of steam and fuel in fire engines. In return for his financial help, Roebuck took a two-thirds share of the patent.

Unfortunately, Roebuck was running into cash difficulties and was unable to finance further development, so Watt shelved his work on steam engines and went to earn a living as a surveyor. A friend of Roebuck, Birmingham factory owner Matthew Boulton (1728–1809), was interested in Watt's engine, not only to pump water at his own factory, but to sell to a wider market. Roebuck tried to sell Boulton part of his patent rights, but the shrewd Boulton wanted more, and sensing Roebuck's difficulties, turned him down.

In 1773 Roebuck went bankrupt, and Boulton took his two-thirds share in the patent in lieu of a £1,200 debt. The following year Watt moved his experimental engine to Boulton's Soho Works in Birmingham and, backed by Boulton, set about full-time development work. In 1775, Boulton the businessman realized that his and Watt's patent was going to expire before they had made any cash from their investment. He petitioned Parliament to extend the patent due to expire in 1783 until 1800. The extension was granted and he and Watt entered into a formal partnership to build and sell engines.

Watt's biggest problem was making a good seal between the piston and the cylinder because there was no means of boring a cylinder to the tolerance Watt needed. However, John Wilkinson (1728–1808), an ironmaster at New Willey, had patented a device to bore cannon barrels to great accuracy (for that time). Watt asked Wilkinson to bore cylinders for him using the new invention, and was able to obtain a good seal using rings of hemp soaked in tallow. As a result, his new experimental engine worked extremely well. He wrote: 'The fire engine I have invented is now going and answers much better than any other that has yet been made.' The improved engine used less than a third of the amount of coal that was normal at that time. Later, Watt built an engine with a cylinder 38 inches (0.97m) in diameter to blow air in one of Wilkinson's blast furnaces. The blower made such an improvement to the furnace that within four years Wilkinson had bought another three engines to blow other furnaces, and ironmasters all over the country adopted the idea.

In 1776, Boulton & Watt's first commercial engine, with a cylinder 50 inches (1.27 m) in diameter, started to pump water at Bloomfield Colliery, Tipton, shortly followed by the one built for John Wilkinson to blow air into the blast furnaces at his ironworks. Soon enquiries poured in from Cornwall, where the tin mines were deep and flooded easily. Coal, not mined locally but bought from distant collieries, was expensive and the cost of running a Newcomen engine limited – for commercial reasons – the depth to which a mine could be operated. Cornish mine owners were keen to in-

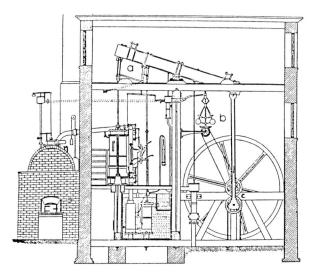

In Watt's double-acting engine, steam is admitted to each side of the piston in turn, an advantage if rotary motion is to be achieved. The picture also shows the parallel motion (a), the governor (b), and the sun-and-planet drive (c) to the flywheel.

crease efficiency, and by 1800 they were working 55 Boulton & Watt engines. Business was so good that Watt's assistant, William Murdock (1754–1839), was permanently employed in Cornwall from 1780 to 1799, and Watt himself spent so much time there that he bought a house in the area. In other parts of the country, colliery owners were less concerned about saving fuel because they had plenty of it; the capital investment in a new Watt engine was hardly justified.

These engines were fine for pumping, but if steam was to replace the water wheel as a power source, rotary motion was needed. Around 1775, Watt had the idea of a rotative engine that was double-acting – that is, one in which steam is admitted to each side of the piston in turn, doubling its power (and smoothing its delivery). However, he was so tied up with the pumping engine business that he had little time to spare for development work. He returned to the problem later and, in 1779, was experimenting with an engine using a crank driven by two single-acting pistons. It was then that he found that the crank – which he had considered to be unpatentable – had been patented by a rival, James Pickard, who had been told about it by one of Watt's workmen. Angered by this, and spurred on by Boulton who saw that the future lay in the double-

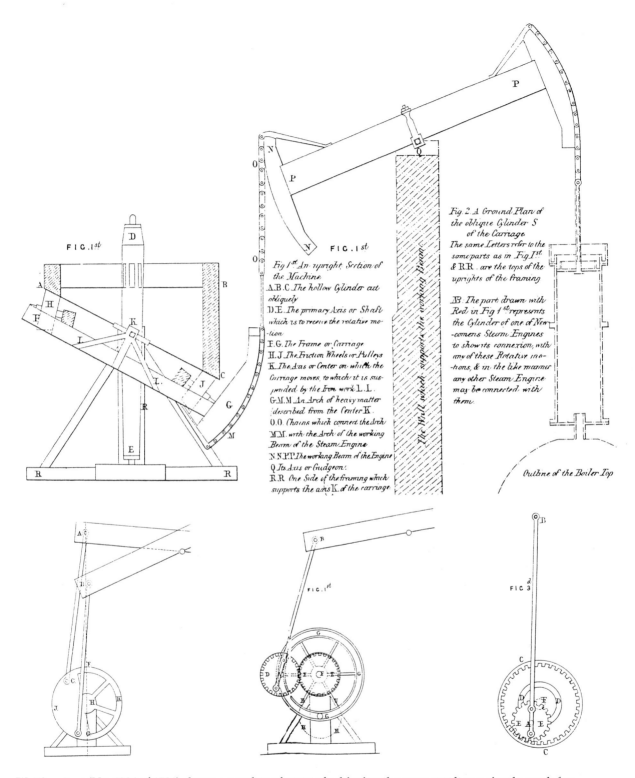

Watt's patent (No. 1306 of 1781) shows a number of ways of achieving the same result as a simple crank for converting reciprocating (backwards and forwards) motion to rotary (round and round) motion – including the sun-and-planet gearing, which he later adopted.

acting rotative engine, Watt developed several alternative methods for getting rotary drive from steam engines, patenting the epicyclic or sun-and-planet gear in 1781.

The double-acting engine implied a rigid connection between piston and beam in order to apply power to the beam on the upward stroke. This introduced a further problem – the end of a rigid connecting rod attached to the end of the beam would move through an arc as the beam went up and down, which would prevent a seal from being made around the connecting rod where it passed through the top of the cylinder. Watt solved this problem by introducing his parallel motion linkage, patented in 1784. Another advance was the centrifugal governor of 1787, which regulated the speed of the engine, though Watt merely adapted this idea from its use in flour mills. Apart from a few refinements, the design of the double-action rotative steam engine of 1784 remained about the same for 60 years.

In 1785 a spinning mill at Papplewick in Nottinghamshire became the first steam-driven factory powered by a Boulton & Watt rotative engine – though the first factory to have a rotative engine driving machinery was James Pickard's Birmingham button factory. In due course the number of steam-powered factories grew; now that they were not reliant on water power, the only reason for building adjacent to a waterway was for ease of transport of raw materials and finished goods. Although steam power was of great importance, it must be remembered that there was still a great deal of small-scale industry, most of which never saw a steam engine. Although in theory steam did away with the need for water power, its impact was less widespread than is often thought. But it made economic sense then – as it does today – for factories large and small to be built in groups, rather than being dotted about the landscape.

The arrival of the first Watt engines in Cornwall in 1777 caused consternation among the local engineers, and tested their ingenuity during the following 23 years as they devised ways of circumventing Watt's patent. In the 1780s and 90s at least twelve engines were built by inventors and other adventurous individuals which might be said to have infringed Boulton and Watt's patent. In 1793, they were eventually provoked into taking action against Edward Bull who,

with Richard Trevithick, had erected an engine at a mine in Cornwall in 1792. After six years of litigation, Boulton and Watt won, and started to collect more than £30,000 in royalty arrears from the patent infringers and other customers who had suspended their payments until the outcome of the court action. This made them pretty unpopular in Cornwall and they sold no more engines there.

One tends to picture Boulton & Watt building and testing steam engines at their Soho Works, and sending out kits of parts to order. However, the reality was that someone wanting a steam engine would send for an engineer, who would size up the need and then go away and prepare drawings of a suitable machine. The engineer would co-ordinate the assembly of parts and construction, but the customer would be responsible for preparing the site, building the engine house, and so on. Many of the parts would be supplied direct by specialist manufacturers – notably the precision cylinders from John Wilkinson's Works. Some of the smaller, more intricate parts would be supplied from the Soho Foundry. If the customer asked, Boulton & Watt would send a fitter, but he would be paid by the customer. Boulton & Watt made their money primarily from royalties, not from selling engines.

As late as 1795, they had no one factory building the 300 engines they supplied that year. However, the supply of parts began to present problems, so in 1796 they decided to set up the Soho Foundry to make every part needed. Ten of the 25 engines they supplied in the year ending October 1797 were built at Soho. But they had

Richard Trevithick (1771–1833).

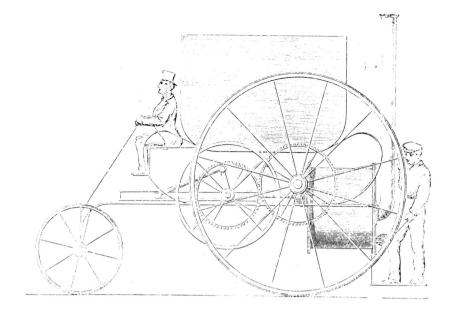

Trevithick's steam-powered carriage, 1803.

left their development rather late, for their patent expired in 1800, by which time they had built some 1,200 steam engines. Watt retired from business a wealthy man, having tripled the efficiency of the steam engine. Now that Boulton & Watt's financial interest in Cornwall had gone, and the company no longer had a representative there, the efficiency of the engines in the area declined as they became poorly maintained.

High-pressure steam

Richard Trevithick (1771–1833) spent his youth immersed in the rivalry between the Cornish engineers and Boulton & Watt. Schooled in engineering by – among others – Watt's assistant, Murdock, by 1795 Trevithick was being paid to make fuel-saving improvements to an engine at Wheal Treasury Mine. Soon after, he was appointed engineer at Ding Dong Mine near Penzance.

Trevithick's ambitions lay in the direction of high-pressure steam – something that Watt refused to consider applying on account of the dangers he foresaw. While Watt was refining his engine (working at pressures below 10 pounds per square inch (69 kPa)), Trevithick spent the 1790s experimenting with models of his own design. On the expiration of Boulton and Watt's patent in 1800, Trevithick built a double-acting high-pressure engine for Cook's Kitchen Mine. This design soon became known as a 'puffer' because the expansion of the high-pressure steam made far more noise than the low-pressure steam in a condensing engine.

In 1801 Trevithick completed the construction of a carriage driven by steam, which conveyed the first passengers ever moved by that motive force. The following year he took out a patent: *Improvements in the construction and application of steam engines*, covering both stationary and road locomotive engines. Next, he built an experimental pumping engine at Coalbrookdale using steam at an unprecedented 145 pounds per square inch (1 MPa). People who saw it were astonished at its small size in comparison to its power output because they were used to seeing huge, ponderous low-pressure engines.

In 1804 a Trevithick steam locomotive was successfully run in Wales on a track between the Pen-y-darran Ironworks and the Glamorganshire Canal. It incorporated the idea of disposing of the exhaust steam by blowing it up the chimney; the unforseen effect of this was to increase the amount of air drawn over the fire in the grate, thus increasing the amount of heat given by the fire. Trevithick failed to realize the significance of this idea, and so did not patent it. Had he done so, he might well have had a great deal of control over the subsequent development of the steam locomotive.

Trevithick's most successful engine was the 'Cornish' type, which used steam at a pressure of 40 pounds per square inch (275 kPa) admitted above a piston to force it down and provide power to pump water. Although more expensive to build than a Watt

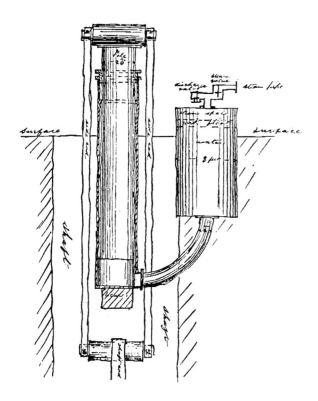

for many years, the only improvement being made by John McNaught, who added a short-stroke high-pressure cylinder to drive the beam half way between its centre and the connecting rod – a so-called compound engine.

With the American expertise in harnessing water power, steam engines were rare in the United States until the middle of the 19th century. The first Newcomen-type engine was imported from England and set up at the Schuyler copper mine in New Jersey in 1754. It was said to have cost £3,000, and was not working until 18 months after the delivery of the parts. It drained the mine of 200,000 gallons (760 kl) a day for 50 years. It was another 20 years before another was erected, to pump the water supply in New York City; a third followed to drain a mine near Providence, RI, in 1780. As in Britain, pumping mines was the first American application of steam power. Later, most American steam effort was directed towards boats for inland waterways (see page 34).

Trevithick's plunger pole engine was simple. A piston in a cylinder was driven up by steam at 100 pounds per square inch (700 kPa). The piston extended outside the cylinder and had a cross-piece attached to its end. Each end of the cross-piece was connected by rods to another cross-bar below the cylinder. The bottom cross-bar was attached to a pumping-rod which was lifted and then dropped by the action of the steam on the piston. However, the plunger pole was neither reliable nor successful; sealing the piston against the cylinder at such a pressure was difficult, and the bore soon became worn. The drawing is from Trevithick's sketch book.

engine, it was more efficient and cheaper to run, and gained favour in the Cornish tin mines where coal was expensive. Not knowing what a great success the 'Cornish' engine would become, Trevithick also built another type of pumping engine called the 'plunger pole' which used steam at 100 pounds per square inch (670 kPa). Although extremely simple and efficient for its day, the plunger pole engine was unsuccessful.

For heavy pumping work, Trevithick's 'Cornish' engine was not bettered for most of the 19th century. For large factories, Watt's rotative engine reigned supreme

Other, smaller, types of engine were built, but they were developments of existing ideas. Easton and Amos's grasshopper engine of 1861 was so called because of the motion of the beam, which is pivoted at its right-hand end rather than in the middle.

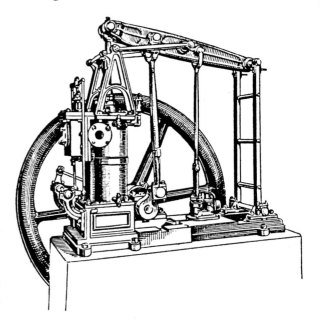

Iron and steel

Smelting and working metals, and particularly iron, is an art which dates back over 3,000 years. Until the beginning of the 18th century, heating iron ore with charcoal in a small furnace or on a hearth, using bellows to raise the temperature, produced enough iron for the needs of smiths, millwrights and the few other users of that material.

Now we see another example of cause and effect: the growing demand for iron as a result of increasing industrialization, and the need to find new ways of extracting it because of an increasing shortage of fuel. In Britain, wood began to run out during the 18th century; in the United States, the shortage was not felt by the iron industry until about 1840 – by which time the demand for coal was increasing anyway.

New fuels

Growing industrialization led to increasing amounts of wood to produce charcoal for smelting iron being needed. The growing population also needed more and more wood for domestic fuel. Wood was being used up far faster than trees could be replaced. The shortage of wood pushed its price up, driving the development of a process using coal to smelt iron. It was found that coal itself could not be used in the traditional furnaces, because its sulphur content made the iron brittle and useless. Coke, however, showed more promise because much of the sulphur in the coal was driven off in the coking process.

Coke was made by heating coal confined in cast-iron 'retorts' in the absence of oxygen, a process known as 'destructive distillation'. The heat drove off many of the compounds in the coal, including methane gas and tar, leaving a mass of carbon containing few impurities. In 1727 Stephen Hale stated that coal yielded inflammable air on being heated in a closed vessel, but it was not until 1782 that Lord Dundonald lit rooms at Culross Abbey with gas from his tar ovens. Ten years later William Murdock lit his house at Redruth in Cornwall with what was now called coal gas. In 1805–07 Murdock built a gas works supplying the cotton mill of Phillips and Lee that proved the commercial viability of coal gas for illumination. The cost of lighting was reduced to less than one third of that for candles, and safety and efficiency increased. At first, coal gas users had their own plant, but as the demand grew gas works were built and pipes of cast iron or lead were laid to serve their areas. Coke from the gas works was used in the iron industry, and the other by-product – coal tar – provided a raw material for the chemical industry.

The blast furnace

For smelting, coke had advantages over charcoal other than price: it was stronger so that the furnace could be stacked higher, smelting more iron at one time and, because a stronger blast could be used with the more robust coke, the furnace became hotter so that the iron became more fluid and could be cast in finer moulds.

In 1709, Abraham Darby I (1677–1717) of Coalbrookdale became the first person to use coke for smelting iron successfully. Darby's iron foundry cast fine wares such as thin-walled cooking pots which were superior to those of his competitors – though his success is attributed in part to the low sulphur content of the coal in that area. Darby's smelting technique did not spread for many years. Ironmasters who produced high-quality iron which could be shaped by rolling and hammering saw Darby's ideas as inappropriate to their particular product and did not adopt the use of coke until the mid-1700s.

Steel is a form of iron containing between 0.7% and 1.7% of carbon. It had been known for a long time but there were great problems in producing material with consistent carbon content in reasonable quantities. Blister steel, produced in the early 1700s, had more carbon at the surface than at the core. In 1740 Benjamin Huntsman (1704–1776) remelted bars of blister steel in

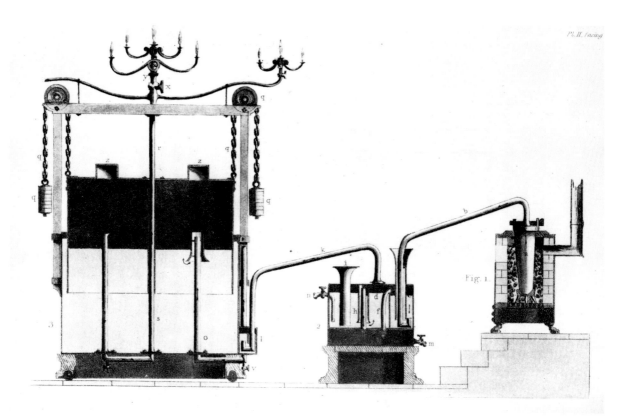

Pl. II. facing

Fig. 1.

Above

Early 19th-century coal-gas plant. The coal is heated in the absence of air ('destructively distilled') in the vessel on the right. The products of distillation pass through the pipe to the condenser (centre), where coal tar products are deposited. The coal gas passes to the expandable gas holder on the left, which feeds the chandeliers on top.

Right

An old type of blast furnace in which a mixture of coke, limestone and iron ore is fired to produce iron, which is run out into the moulds seen in the foreground. The arrangement of the moulds gave rise to the name 'pig iron'. The pigs are joined to the sow; see Figure opposite.

a closed crucible to produce a cast steel of uniform carbon content and free of mineral impurities, or 'slag'. This was known as crucible steel, but it could not be produced in large quantities because of the method. Not until the Bessemer process, invented in 1855 and refined thereafter, was steel available in sufficient quantities for it to be used for making things other than knife blades and similar small articles.

Coke-produced pig iron was not suitable for beating into wrought iron because it contained too many impurities which made it brittle and prone to crumble under the hammer. The first person to develop a method of converting coke-produced pig iron to wrought iron is said to be Abraham Darby II (1711–1763) in the middle 1700s; however, he left no records as to how his process worked. The first to record a successful process – and indeed patent it – was Henry Cort (1740–1800) of Fontly Forge (near Fareham in Hampshire) in 1784. Cort melted the iron in a coal-burning 'reverberatory' furnace – in which the heat from the burning coal was reflected from a sloping roof on to the charge of pig iron. When molten, the iron was 'puddled' – stirred with an iron bar to bring it into contact with the air; the carbon in the pig iron burnt away, leaving malleable iron. Because the coal was separated from the charge it did not contaminate it. The base of the furnace was lined with sand, some of which reacted with the iron charge thereby reducing the yield. Puddled iron – though still inferior to charcoal-smelted iron – was acceptable and demand for it grew. In the previous year, Cort had also patented his grooved rollers which were used to roll the puddled iron into bars, during which more impurities were squeezed out of the iron.

In the early 1800s the losses in puddling were avoided by lining the furnace with iron oxide instead of sand. Oxygen from the oxide combined with the carbon in the molten iron, which it agitated as it bubbled out, thereby precluding the need to stir it. This new process was termed 'wet puddling' as opposed to Cort's dry puddling.

John 'Iron-Mad' Wilkinson, patentee in 1774 of the cannon-boring mill which had been so important to James Watt, obtained large armament orders from the

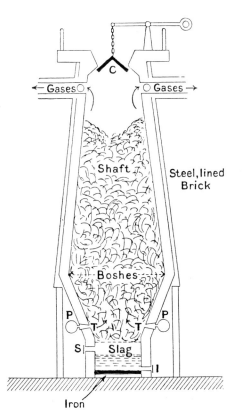

Electromagnet lifting sow and pigs from the sand mould.

Left
Section of a blast furnace. The air blast is blown through 'tuyères' marked T on the diagram, from an annular pipe P. Molten slag is drawn off at S and molten iron at I. The feed mixture of coke, limestone and iron ore is introduced through the cup-and-cone C. The widest part of the furnace is the 'boshes'.

The bridge across the River Severn between Benthall and Madeley Wood (now Ironbridge) was opened to traffic on New Year's Day 1781. Designed and built by a team led by Abraham Darby III (1750–1791), it consisted entirely of iron members cast in open sand moulds at the Coalbrookdale works. No bolts or rivets were used in the construction; the parts were wedged together or held with dovetail joints. This, the world's first iron bridge, still stands and is now used by pedestrians visiting the Ironbridge Gorge Museum.

The bridge has a total length of 196 feet (59.7 m), a span of 100 feet 6 inches (30.6 m) and a rise of 50 feet (15.2 m). The five main cast-iron ribs, each cast in two pieces and weighing $5\frac{3}{4}$ tons with masonry abutments, support a carriageway 24 feet (7.3 m) carried on open sand-cast iron plates $2\frac{1}{2}$ inches (63 mm) thick. The total weight of cast iron in the bridge is 378.5 tons.

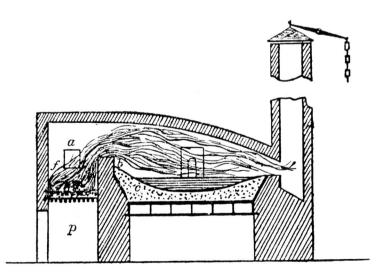

This section of a reverbatory furnace shows how the heat from the fire on the left is reflected down on to the molten metal by the shaped roof before escaping up the chimney on the right.

government. Many of the cannon used in the Franco–British Peninsular War (1808–1814) – so called because it was fought on the Iberian Peninsula – were machined by him. In 1787 Wilkinson launched the first iron barge which he had built to carry castings down the River Severn from his Coalbrookdale works. He built the first steam-driven forge hammer in 1782. As well as his interest in iron – from which he built a sizeable personal fortune – Wilkinson ran a large farm near Wrexham, and experimented there with steam-driven machinery. He lived up to his nickname to the last for, when he died in 1808, he was laid to rest in an iron coffin.

In iron and steel production, developments in the United States were never far behind those in Britain. Pennsylvania is a state of great mineral wealth – particularly iron ore and coal (not to mention the oil and natural gas which, in 1859, caused as much excitement as the Californian gold rush). It was here that, in 1783, three Scottish brothers built a blast-furnace, thus laying the foundation of the great iron industries that were to develop there. Another Scottish immigrant, Andrew Carnegie, introduced the Bessemer process for manufacturing steel in 1868, very soon after its invention.

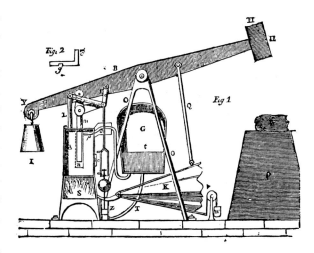

Steam forge-hammer. The thicker the workpiece, the less the impact.

Henry Bessemer's patent (No. 578 of 1860) for making steel. The barrel is charged with molten iron, and air blown through it to burn off the carbon. The charge is then tipped out of the barrel – hence the shape of the spout.

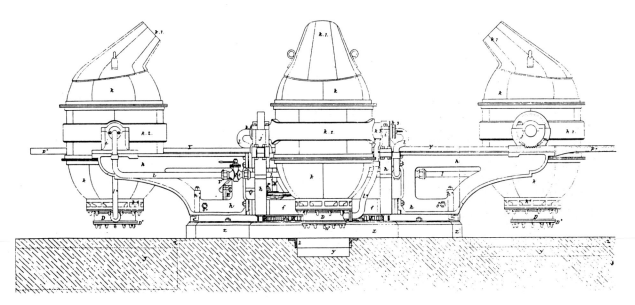

21

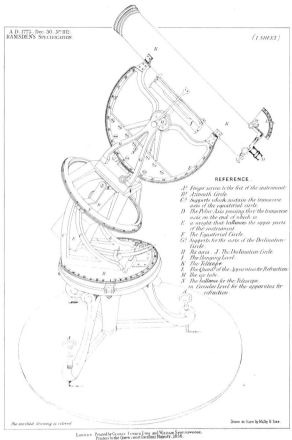

A.D. 1775. Dec. 30. Nº 1112.
RAMSDEN'S SPECIFICATION.

(1 SHEET)

REFERENCE.

A⁸ *Finger screws to the feet of the instrument*
B⁸ *Azimuth Circle.*
C⁸ *Supports which sustain the transverse axis of the equaterial circle.*
D *The Polar Axis passing thro' the transverse axis on the end of which is*
E *a weight that ballances the upper parts of the instrument.*
F *The Equaterial Circle.*
G⁸ *Supports for the axis of the Declination Circle.*
H *Its axis . J. The Declination Circle.*
I *The Hanging Level.*
K *The Telescope*
L *The Quad.⁸ of the Apparatus for Refraction*
M *The eye tube.*
N *The ballance for the Telescope.*
   in Circular Level for the apparatus for refraction.

The inrolled drawing is colored

Drawn on Stone by Malby & Sons.

LONDON Printed by GEORGE EDWARD EYRE and WILLIAM SPOTTISWOODE, Printers to the Queen's most Excellent Majesty. 1856.

18th century precision engineering: one of Jesse Ramsden's astronomical measuring instruments (Patent No. 1112 of 1795).

Left
Nasmyth's steam hammer at work.

Forging

Iron is frequently shaped by heating and hammering – or forging. Originally, this was done by the blacksmith under the spreading chestnut tree; as workpieces became more massive, mechanical means were developed.

The horse chestnut is so called because it was used from the 16th century for treating respiratory diseases in horses – hence its frequent proximity to the forge, for the smith was responsible for more than shoeing.

Early forge hammers were worked by a rotating cam which lifted and dropped a hammer on to an anvil, but there were problems with this: the hammer's lift was small – typically 18 inches (45cm) – so that the thicker a piece of metal, the less the fall. Because the lift was always the same, it was not possible to vary the blow; moreover, the face of the hammer was parallel to the anvil only at one point. A large amount of energy was wasted converting steam (or water) power to the rotary motion of the cam and then to the rise and fall of the hammer.

In 1839 James Nasmyth (1808–1890), an engineer from Manchester, received a letter from someone who had an order to forge a shaft three feet (0.914 m) in diameter for a steamer's paddle wheels. There was at that time no forge hammer in Britain that could carry out the work, and the writer wanted Nasmyth to design a hammer to do it. Within a few minutes, he conceived a hammer wherein steam lifted a piston which was effectively part of the hammer, which then dropped when the steam supply was cut off and the cylinder vented. Later versions used steam to assist the hammer downwards. Not only could the hammer be lifted to a greater height; that height was variable, making the steam hammer a useful and versatile tool. As a demonstration of the fine control that could be achieved, a skilled operator would place a watch on the anvil with a moist wafer on it. The hammer was lowered on to the wafer which stuck to its face; then raised without damaging the watch. Steam hammers were built in many sizes with the largest weighing many tons. They could work much larger billets of metal than was previously possible, and made an essential contribution to heavy engineering of the time.

In the iron industry, James Beaumont Neilson (1792–1865) had been experimenting with heating the blast that was fed into furnaces. In 1828 he patented the idea and the first practical hot-blast furnace was set up at the Clyde works in 1832. The effects speak for themselves: in 1829 each ton of iron produced needed over seven and a half tons of coal; in 1833 this was reduced to just under three tons. Within three years the hot blast had been accepted by the industry and its use was widespread.

Mining

Until the application of steam-powered pumps, the depth of mines of all types was restricted by flooding. It was impracticable to use huge teams of animals to power pumps so that the mine could be driven ever deeper, and much unmined wealth therefore lay beyond the grasp of the mineowners. Powerful and tireless, steam enabled vast new reserves to be opened up, and its use spread rapidly in the mining industry.

In older, shallower mines, there had been no special provision for ventilation. But the build-up of poisonous and explosive gases as workings became deeper and more extensive led to the necessity for ventilation. The first measure was to make two 'roads' into the mine; one to allow the air in to be circulated around the mine before it was vented through the other. The circulation was encouraged by placing fires or heated rocks in the out-flow road, so that the warmed air would rise up the shaft and out of the mine, drawing more air in to replace it. Later, systems of doors and partitions were used within the tunnels to ensure the air-flow was not short-circuited in its route.

In 1807 the first mechanical mine ventilator was installed at Hebburn Colliery. It consisted of a square wooden piston working in a wood-lined cylinder, pumping some 6,000 cubic feet (168m^3) of air per minute into the workings. Other pumps were devised; one such was Struvé's ventilator, a large iron bell with inlet and outlet valves, moving up and down in a tank of water.

Even with mine ventilation, many fatal explosions were caused by miners' candles igniting gas accumulations and clouds of fine coal dust. One method used to clear explosive gas was to send one man – a 'fireman' – ahead with a candle attached to the end of a long pole. The fireman was wrapped in damp sackcloth. Dressed thus, he would make his way to the coalface, keeping the candle close to the floor of the tunnel, away from explosive gas which accumulated in the tops of the tunnels. On reaching the coalface, the fireman covered

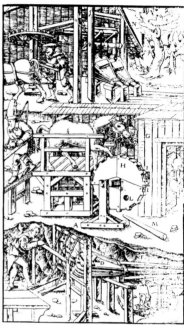

Left

The 'man engine'. As well as pumping water, steam engines lowered men down the mine, and raised them at the end of the shift. Foot and hand holds were attached to the pumping rod and the wall of the mine at intervals determined by the stroke of the pump. To come up, a miner would step on to the lowest foothold and wait for the pumping rod to change its direction of travel whereupon he would be hoisted upwards. As the rod reached its upper limit, the foothold would draw level with the fixed foothold on to which he would step and wait for the pumping rod to go down again, bringing within his range another foothold that would carry him yet further upwards until he reached the surface. As can be imagined, it was highly dangerous.

Right

Ventilating a mine with bellows.

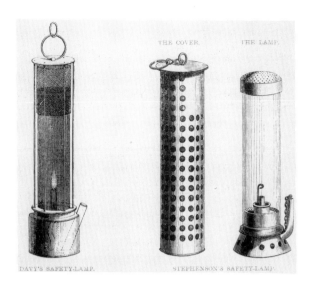

DAVY'S SAFETY-LAMP.   STEPHENSON'S SAFETY-LAMP.

Both George Stephenson and Humphry Davy addressed the problem of safe miners' lamps, and produced similar solutions. Stephenson's lamp (*right*) was widely used in his home county of Northumberland, where it became known as the 'Geordie lamp' after its inventor. Natives of Tyneside are still called 'Geordies'.

his face with the wet sacking, and raised the candle to ignite any gas which had accumulated. Once this was done, the brave man was joined by his colleagues who could get to work.

Another idea was to do away with the candle, and derive illumination from the phosphorescent glow of rotting fish. However, this provided insufficient light, and the smell was unpopular with the miners.

With the increase in mine-depth, fatal explosions became so frequent that in 1815 the Sunderland Society for Preventing Accidents in Coal Mines asked Sir Humphry Davy (1778–1829) to look into the problem. He set to work and discovered that the flame of a methane–air mixture could not travel through gauze. His first safety lamp was tested early the following year and found to work effectively. The Newcastle miner and enginewright George Stephenson discovered the same principle and produced his own safety lamp – known as the 'Geordie' lamp – at the same time as Davy's. The safety lamp was improved over the years but the basic principle remained the same.

Mining requires three activities: prospecting, reaching the material, and getting it out. Miners had long sought ways to mechanize their work, but there was little progress during our period. After handwork, rocks were split by fire and water; then by gunpowder in shot holes. Trevithick is accredited with inventing the first mechanical rock-boring machine for use in mines (1813), but its success was limited by the softness of its drill bit. Significant advances were prompted in the second half of the 19th century by the spread of the railways, with the application of compressed air to drills used in the construction of the Mont Cenis and Simplon tunnels through the Alps in Europe and the five-mile-long Hoosac Tunnel in northwestern Massachusetts.

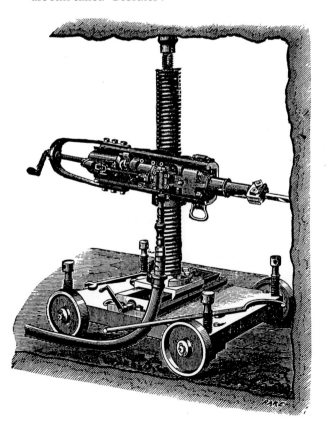

The rock drill invented by Charles Burleigh of Massachusetts was powered by compressed air at 80 pounds per square inch (550 kPa).

Transport

Roads

The state of the roads in England was abominable until the late 18th century. Generally uneven, roads might consist of seas of mud, water-filled ruts often many feet deep, enormous stones and other hazards conspiring to make any journey unpleasant, if not impossible. The best way of getting from one place to another was to walk; the best way to move goods was by pack horse.

There were certainly no regular, year-round coach services at the beginning of the 18th century; the roads were too bad for that. Neither was there much incentive for local people, who were not used to going anywhere, to improve their roads, let alone to improve them for others. However, in Britain there was a growing movement towards Turnpike Trusts; groups of people adopted a stretch of road and then charged its users by taking money at a toll house at each end. The first turnpike, on the Great North Road between London and Edinburgh, had been set up in 1663. Between 1720 and 1730, 71 Turnpike Acts were passed, and 100 years later 20,000 miles of road were administered by 3,783 Turnpike Trusts. But a Trust had no obligation to improve its road, though that was supposed to be the purpose of the tolls. Improvement needed both techniques for making and surfacing roads, and the public demand for them, and both gradually had their effect.

The first road builder was John Metcalf – Blind Jack of Knaresborough (1717–1810) – who (though blind from the age of six) knew the Yorkshire ways intimately and developed a method of laying a good, well-drained foundation for a cambered surface which could drain into roadside ditches. An extraordinary man, Metcalf was an indefatigable traveller, who once walked from London to Harrogate in six days, two days less than it took Colonel Liddel who offered him a lift in his coach for the same journey. Metcalf set up a vehicle hire business, brought fish from the coast to sell in the Leeds district, acted as a recruiting sergeant for General Wade's army in the Jacobite rebellion of 1745,

Blind Jack of Knaresborough – John Metcalf (1717–1810).

The 'Father of Civil Engineering' – Thomas Telford (1757–1834).

Telford's suspension bridge (1819–25) over the Menai Straits between mainland Wales and the Isle of Anglesey is 1710 feet (521 m) long.

imported clothes from Aberdeen and set up as a carrier before turning to roadmaking.

In 1765, a Turnpike Act empowered a Harrogate–Boroughbridge road, of which Metcalf offered to build a three mile stretch. His offer accepted, he sold his carrying business and built the road to the contractor's complete satisfaction. Over the next 30 years Metcalf continued to build many stretches of Yorkshire roads, some – such as the Huddersfield–Manchester road – crossing bogs on bundles of heather. His total achievement was about 180 miles.

But it was Thomas Telford (1757–1834), the so-called 'Father of Civil Engineering', who made road building a new science. Like the later builders of railways, he saw the merit of a reasonably level line, and his masterpiece was the London–Holyhead road, now the A5, with its magnificent suspension bridge over the Menai Straits (illustrated above).

John Loudon McAdam (1756–1836) made his contribution to roadmaking by concentrating on methods for producing a well-drained surface. McAdam showed early ability as a road builder; while at school he constructed a model section of the road between Maybole and Kirkoswald. In the 1790s, as a road trustee at an estate in Ayrshire, he decided to do something about the roads in the area, which were in a sorry condition. His proposed solution was to rebuild them with layers of broken stone – each piece weighing no more than six ounces (170 g) – raised above the surrounding land, with drainage ditches either side to keep the foundation dry. The passage of time and traffic would compact the layers of stone to form a firm hard surface – a 'macadam' surface. McAdam's well-drained road, with its compacted layers, precluded the

A comment on seven years of wear on a road in Hyde Park.

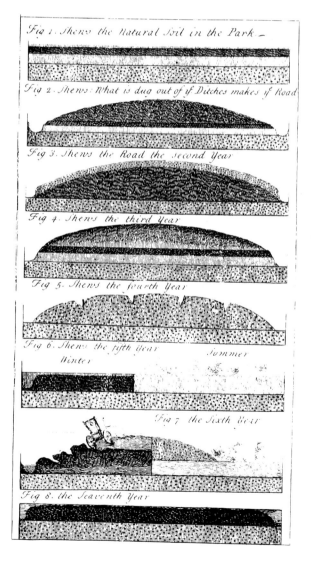

Fig 1. Shews the Natural Soil in the Park.

Fig 2. Shews What is dug out of if Ditches makes if Road

Fig 3. Shews the Road the second Year

Fig 4. Shews the third Year

Fig 5. Shews the fourth Year

Fig 6. Shews the fifth Year
Winter   Summer

Fig 7. the Sixth Year

Fig 8. the Seaventh Year

need for expensive, solid, hand-laid foundations, which were designed to prevent the soil underneath from turning to mud whenever it rained.

McAdam was able to try out his proposed improvements when, in 1815, he became Surveyor-General of the Bristol roads. His work was successful enough to warrant his publishing *A Practical Essay on the Scientific Repair and Preservation of Roads* in 1819.

In 1827 McAdam was appointed general surveyor of roads and his road improvements helped build the network of routes which encouraged the development of business communications before the railway system expanded. Although later surfaces were bound together with tar – hence 'tarmacadam' – McAdam himself didn't use that material. Thus McAdam's name – and, more important, his techniques – passed into the language on both sides of the Atlantic.

Better roads ushered in the age of the coach. We tend to think of the coach and four spanking along the highway as an age-old means of transport, but roads were not improved until after many of the canals were built and the railway was beginning to become practicable. By then, the coach was almost superfluous, but lasted long enough to give us those fine Christmas-card images of the golden days of travel that hardly were.

Waterways

Even with improved roads, the only practical way of moving goods was by water, but this was not widely exploited at first because there was no tradition of that sort of commerce. One of the first materials to be moved by water was coal – from Newcastle to London. Even though London was comparatively rural, it could not rely on wood as fuel, and needed its coal.

Initially, the many navigable rivers were improved; then, in 1761, the Duke of Bridgewater opened a canal to move his coal from Worsley to Manchester. At the pit mouth, a horse-load of coal (280 lb (127 kg)) cost 10*d*. By the time the load reached Manchester, the price was more than double, and there was no more economical way of moving it for, even if it were sent by the Mersey Navigation Company at 3*s*4*d* per ton, it still had to be taken to and from the boats. A far-sighted man, the Duke decided to build his own canal, and he and his agent John Gilbert called in the millwright James Brindley (1716–1772) to survey possible courses and

The Cambridge Mail Telegraph outside the White
Horse Tavern and Family Hotel, London about 1828.

The 'Father of the Canals' – James Brindley
(1716–1772).

superintend the works. The Acts for the canal were passed in 1759 and 1760. The most formidable part of the undertaking was the Barton Aqueduct over the River Irwell; 200 yards (183m) long, it takes the canal 39 feet (11.8m) above the river in three main spans. At the time it was 'a bold and ingenious enterprise' – and remains so, for no one had attempted anything like it before. At the Worsley end, the canal was driven into the hill to meet the mine workings so that the coals could be readily loaded. Brindley's tunnel was about a mile in length, but the system was later extended to become an underground system of some 40 miles (64.4 km). Brindley also laid down a tramway in the mine to make it easier to move the coal from the face, and designed cranes at both ends of the canal for loading and unloading. At the Manchester end, the canal was driven into a hillside, and a crane driven by a water-wheel raised the boxes of coal up a vertical shaft to the surface for sale.

Building the Bridgewater Canal nearly bankrupted the Duke, but his faith in the investment – and in his engineer – was justified for, with coals for sale in Manchester at 5s10d per ton, he gradually recouped his fortune. His income was £3,100,000 per year in 1800, and when he died three years later his art collection alone was said to be worth £150,000*.

Brindley continued to build canals for the Duke, and dreamt of the day when the main British rivers – the Thames, Severn, Trent and Mersey – would be linked

*We have not attempted to express sums of money in modern terms, for any conversion is largely meaningless. Suffice it to say that the Duke was not poor, even by today's standards, and that his efforts enabled him to bring down the price of coal over a wide area.

The Barton Aqueduct carries the Bridgewater Canal over the River Irwell in Lancashire.

Pont Cysyllte Aqueduct takes the Llangollen canal across the River Dee. The channel is of cast iron, little wider than the narrowboats which sail on it. On one side is a footpath with a hand-rail; on the other a sheer drop to the river some 118 feet (36 m) below at low water.

by a canal system. The Grand Trunk Canal linking the Trent and Mersey was proposed by the potter Josiah Wedgwood (1730–1795), supported by the Duke of Bridgewater, and built by Brindley. Wedgwood's need was to move china clay from Cornwall to his works in Staffordshire; the Canal also enabled him to distribute his finished goods.

These successful workings laid the foundation of the canal system that grew in Britain over the next 70 years. Brindley having led the way, other canal builders followed – notably John Rennie (1761–1821) and Thomas Telford. Canal mania gripped the country and hundreds of 'ordinary people' took the opportunity to invest. Some canals prospered; others failed, but by 1830 there was a canal system of 4,000 miles and the most successful companies paid a dividend to their investors of 28 per cent.

Earlier canals were built as cheaply as possible and followed the contours of the land rather than going through cuttings or tunnels, or along embankments. This could make them long and twisty, but boatmen's wages were low so that extra length didn't matter. Telford, who always delivered the best, was appointed as sole engineer and architect of the Ellesmere canal in 1793, after a stint as Surveyor of Public Works for

Shropshire. The canal – to link the rivers Mersey, Dee and Severn – was the most ambitious of its kind at that time, and gave us such marvels as the Pont Cysyllte Aqueduct (1805), whose 19 arches stride 1007 feet (307 m) across the River Dee at a height of 118 feet (36 m) above low water.

Telford was also engineer for the 110 foot (33.5 m) wide Caledonian Canal to link the east and west coasts of Scotland through existing natural lochs. One of the most impressive stretches was 'Neptune's Staircase', a flight of eight giant locks changing the level 90 feet (27.4 m) between Loch Eil and Loch Lochy eight miles distant. The project cost nearly £1M and failed to live up to the commercial success which Telford had predicted – making it the biggest failure of his engineering career.

Telford also improved existing canals, building a new tunnel at Harecastle Hill, Staffordshire, for the Grand Junction Canal, and improvements to the Birmingham Canal. He planned the Gotha Canal in Sweden, which connected the Baltic with the North Sea. For that he received the Swedish order of knighthood.

From 1825 Telford advised canal owners to improve the system in order to make themselves competitive with proposed railway schemes then being mooted. As a result of this advice, he was commissioned to design the Birmingham and Liverpool Junction from the Birmingham Canal at a point near Wolverhampton, to the Mersey at Ellesmere Port. This connection opened a transport link not only from Birmingham to Liverpool, but also to Manchester via the Liverpool to Manchester Canal. The Junction was Telford's last canal project.

Canal boats were pulled by horses or donkeys; steam came into experimental use in the late 1700s. A pioneer of steam-powered boats was William Symington (1763–1831). Symington, a Scottish engineer, patented in 1787 (No 1610) an improved form of steam engine which used chains and ratchet wheels to produce rotary motion. The following year, Symington built a small steam engine for Patrick Miller, who wanted to power a boat with hand-operated paddle wheels. The first experimental boat worked well enough for Miller to ask Symington to make a larger engine for a bigger boat. This one had 18-inch (46 cm) cylinders and was tested in a boat in 1789. Although it

The five-rise staircase locks at Bingley in Yorkshire. To descend, float into the top lock chamber and shut the gate behind you. Let the water down to the level of the second chamber, open the gate in front of you, and float from the first to the second chamber. Shut the gate behind you, let the water down and so on. To ascend, reverse the process.

Right

Water being such a convenient mode of transport, it is not surprising that the United States was developing its needs at about the same time as Britain. A notable feat was the great Erie Canal. Begun in 1816 and completed in 1825, it has a length of 360 miles (580 km) and joins New York's Hudson River to Lake Erie. The upper picture shows the dam at Vischer's Ferry under construction; below is the construction of a lock at Waterford.

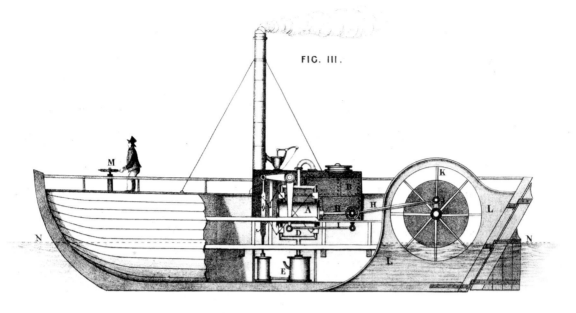

FIG. III.

The steamboat *Charlotte Dundas* .

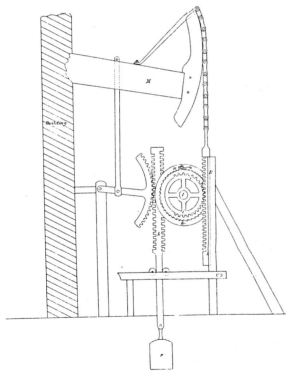

Symington's patent (No. 1610 of 1787), showing a method of converting reciprocating motion to rotary motion by rack, spur gear, ratchet and pawl.

could do seven m.p.h (11.2 km/h), Miller was disenchanted by Symington's crude chain and ratchet drive, and lost interest.

In 1801 the Governor of the Forth and Clyde Canal Company, Lord Dundas, asked Symington to look into the possibility of using steam power on the canal. Symington concluded that his chain and ratchet drive was not particularly good; in 1801 he patented (No 2544) the roller-guided piston rod, which drove a crank via a connecting rod. In 1802 this design was used to power a tug boat, the *Charlotte Dundas*, which was able to tow two barges 19.5 miles (31.4km) into a headwind in six hours.

The third Duke of Bridgewater, impressed by the *Charlotte Dundas*, ordered eight boats of a similar design. Unfortunately the order was cancelled in 1803 after the Duke's death. At the same time, the Forth and Clyde Company discontinued the use of the *Charlotte Dundas* upon discovering the damage that her wake did to the canal banks, and Symington's steam-boat career came to a premature end.

In the United States – not surprisingly – there was a much more receptive attitude to steam-powered boats. Most development effort was directed not to improving the imported design of steam engine, but to adapting it to navigation. In 1806 Robert Fulton (1765–

1815), who had been born in Pennsylvania but had crossed the Atlantic to study in London and Paris, returned to his native land intent on building a steam boat. The following year, he launched his *Clermont* on the Hudson, demonstrating by his 150-mile (240 km) maiden voyage from Albany to New York City and back in 62 hours that steam navigation had arrived.

Within weeks, he was running the world's first commercial navigation operation, and had started to add to his fleet. The following year, John Stevens and his son Robert, of Hoboken, NJ, launched the first of their commercial-scale steamboats. And in 1812, the first western river steamboat of the Fulton group, built at Pittsburgh, inaugurated steam navigation in the trans-Appalachian West. Fulton's achievement must be set in further context. When he built *Clermont*, there were only about a dozen steam engines in the whole of the United States; five years after his death, the French sent Jean Baptiste Marestier, a leading naval engineer, to look into the growth of steam navigation in America.

As the canal network grew in Britain, people became used to the idea of moving raw materials and goods; the canals ushered in a new era of commerce. However, there had been no overall planning, and while some locks were broad enough to take barges, others would take only the narrowboats – just under seven foot (2 m) wide – as they do today. This limited cargo size – and at busy times there were many hold-ups at the locks. Altogether, canals were slow, and because there was no competition the operators charged high prices. Cotton brought to Liverpool from America, for onward transmission to Manchester for processing in the mills, often had to wait weeks at the docks – indeed, it took longer to reach Manchester from Liverpool than it did to cross the Atlantic.

Manufactured goods suffered the same problems in reverse, having to wait to be taken to the docks in Liverpool. The trade route set up by the Duke of Bridgewater's Manchester–Liverpool canal had encouraged growth in the two areas but was now unable

Robert Fulton's sketches of 1793, in which he worked out the principles of the paddle-steamer.

Robert Fulton's 1802 prophecy of steam navigation on the Hudson River – the title page of his notebook.

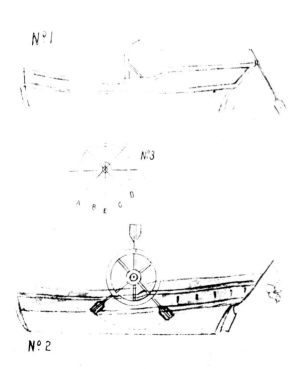

to serve them adequately. Sometimes boats were held up altogether when the canals froze over. Merchants suffered from such delays, but the canal operators didn't care because they had a monopoly on transporting heavy items; horse-drawn carts had been tried on the Liverpool–Manchester route but were unsatisfactory. Besides, canal owners had a backlog of work and they could charge what they wanted. Inland waterways, had they but known it, carried the seeds of their own destruction.

The railways

The idea of a railway, or tramway as it was called originally – a smooth track upon which wheeled vehicles run easily – goes back hundreds of years. Such tracks were laid in and around mines, with humans and animals pulling the wagons. At the end of the 17th century, Sir Humphrey Mackworth in Glamorgan tried fitting his coal wagons with sails but, as may be imagined, the results were far from satisfactory.

At the beginning of the 19th century, Murdock and Trevithick – both in Cornwall – had experimented with steam locomotives. Trevithick brought his *Catch-me-who-can* and passenger wagons to London in 1808,

Trevithick's steam locomotive *Catch-me-who-can* being demonstrated in London, 1808.

Timothy Hackworth's *Wylam Dilly*, generally known as William Hedley's *Puffing Billy*.

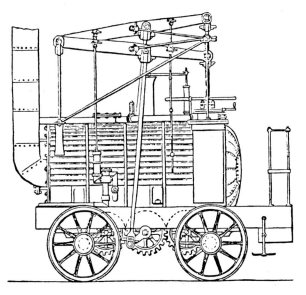

and charged people one shilling to ride round a circular track on a site in front of the present Euston terminus. The experiment was hardly a financial success and, when a rail broke and the locomotive overturned, Trevithick abandoned it.

This was a pity, because the time was ripe for locomotive development and, had he persevered, Trevithick might well have become the 'father of the railways', a mantle which was to be donned by George Stephenson (1781–1848).

Stephenson was appointed enginewright at Killingworth Colliery in Northumberland in 1812; he had earlier taught himself all about engines by working with them, stripping them down and rebuilding them at the weekends to become privy to their innermost secrets. Meanwhile, a Mr Blackett, the owner of nearby Wylam Colliery – where Stephenson had begun his career – had been experimenting with steam locomotives. His first two were copies of a locomotive design patented by Mr Blenkinsop of Leeds in 1811; in spite of Trevithick's convincing demonstrations that smooth wheels worked on smooth rails, Blenkinsop was still using rack-and-pinion drives – though it must be said that, weight for weight, Blenkinsop's engines could pull a load five times as great as Trevithick's. The difficulty would come if the speed were to be increased.

Blackett then commissioned William Hedley to build what turned out to be a more successful engine, *Wylam Dilly* – better known as *Puffing Billy*. Stephenson spent some time watching the Wylam trials; then, inspired, he built an engine for use at Killingworth. *Blucher*, the first of many Stephenson locomotives, could pull a 30-ton load up a slight incline at four miles per hour (6.4 km/h).

Thus began Stephenson's railway career – the right man in the right place at the right time. In 1821, Parliament approved the construction of a railway from Stockton to Darlington, promoted by Edward Pease. Stephenson heard of this, and invited Pease to see his locomotives at work at Killingworth. Pease was thus converted to the idea of using steam locomotives, rather than horses, to pull the wagons on the projected railway – indeed, he invited Stephenson to survey the line and design the rails. He also lent him some money to set up a locomotive factory at Newcastle.

The Stockton and Darlington Railway was opened on 27 September 1825. Thousands came to see the first

train – six wagons loaded with coal and flour, 21 with seats for passengers, and six more full of coal. A stationary engine was used to haul the train up the Brusselton Incline, after which that first train was attached to *Locomotion* driven by George Stephenson himself, and the train travelled to Stockton at speeds of up to 12 m.p.h. (19.2 km/h); by the time it arrived, about 600 people were hanging on to it.

In spite of this enthusiasm, it was thought that there would be little passenger traffic on the railway, which had been built to carry freight. However, it was soon clear that there was a future for passengers, and Stephenson was asked to design a 'railway carriage'. The *Experiment* was pulled by a horse, and looked like a shed on wheels. It took two hours to travel the 12 miles (19.2 km); the fare was one shilling (5p), and passengers could take up to 14 lbs (6.3 kg) of luggage free.

The railways spread

We left the canal story with a report of the unsatisfactory service between Liverpool and Manchester. In about 1821 a Mr Sandars, a Liverpool merchant,

The opening of the Stockton & Darlington Railway, 27 September 1825. It is not clear whether the leading man on horseback is ceremonial or admonitory.

broached the idea of a railway to join the two cities. A survey was made of the route – with difficulty, as farmers and landowners didn't like the idea of such a thing crossing their land. More than once the surveyors had to flee from angry protesters. The surveyor visited Killingworth to see George Stephenson's engine. Stephenson and his partner Losh wanted their patent to bear fruit, and offered the surveyor a quarter share of any profits derived from the use of their locomotive on any railways constructed south of a line drawn from Liverpool to Hull – which must have seemed a pretty safe offer at the time. However, there were difficulties: the surveyor fell prey to illness and debt, and eventually, George Stephenson was appointed engineer to build the railway. Early in 1824, Sandars had a public declaration drawn up and signed by more than 150 merchants from Liverpool and Manchester setting forth their views: that they considered 'the present establishments for the transport of goods quite inadequate, and that a new line of conveyance has become absolutely necessary to conduct the increasing trade of the country with speed, certainty, and economy.'

The first railway carriage – the *Experiment*.

A committee was appointed to take the necessary measures. In fairness, they met the Duke of Bridgewater's canal agent, Mr Bradshaw, to give the canal company a chance to improve its service. They even invited him to become a shareholder in the new railway scheme. His reply: 'All or none!' was presumably made in the smug assumption that the canal's position as the only means of conveying goods was unassailable. People had talked about it for years and nothing had happened. Besides, the path of the railway crossed Chat Moss, a bog which couldn't support a man, let alone a railway. And the canal owner and his cronies were pretty influential, and no landowner along the way wanted to be disturbed by a railway. No, in Bradshaw's view, the canal was king.

To ensure that they were making the right decision, a group of interested people went to inspect Stephenson's locomotive engines and the unfinished Stockton and Darlington railway, which strengthened their resolve to build a double line of railway between Liverpool and Manchester. They were certain they could provide safe, cheap transport for merchandise between the two towns, which would take five or six

hours instead of 36 hours as by canal.

In January 1825 Stephenson demonstrated his Stockton and Darlington locomotive to a group of committee members and engineers. They saw a locomotive and loaded waggons with a weight of 54 tons travelling at seven m.p.h. (11.2 km/h), and were then borne in a carriage at about 12 m.p.h. (19.2 km/h). Meanwhile a second, more thorough, survey of the Liverpool–Manchester route was being conducted, hampered by the ill will of the canal company and land owners.

When the survey was complete, and the proprietors were preparing to apply to Parliament for an Act to enable them to build the railway, the canal companies sought a reconciliation, promising to use steam vessels, reduce the length of the canal by three miles, and lower the rates. However it was too late, and arrangements were made to proceed with the Bill in the Parliamentary session of 1825. The canal companies set out to fight every inch of the way and disseminated all sorts of propaganda – the railway would prevent cows grazing and hens laying; the smoke would kill birds; cinders would ignite houses; horses would become extinct, so that there would be no market for hay and oats; boilers would explode, killing passengers. After two months of detailed enquiry and examination, the Bill was defeated.

A new route was surveyed avoiding opposing land owners. More capital was raised, principally from the Marquis of Stafford who had an interest in the canal, but who presumably saw the writing on the wall. The Bill was eventually passed in 1828.

In spite of Stephenson's demonstrations to the contrary, there were still armchair pundits who thought it necessary to have teeth on the rails to engage with gears on the engine's wheels. Others thought that the Liverpool–Manchester railway should be worked by stationary engines – 21 of them along the track pulling the trains by cable. Stephenson was adamant, with the result that a prize of £500 was offered for the best prototype locomotive engine to work the railway.

The 'Rainhill Trials' took place on 6 October 1829. There were five entries of which one, Brandreth's (or Winans') *Cycloped*, was disqualified because it was worked by a horse on a treadmill. The other four were Braithwaite and Ericsson's *Novelty*, Hackworth's *Sanspareil*, Burstall's *Perseverance*, and Stephenson's *Rocket*.

The 'Father of the Railways' – George Stephenson (1781–1848).

Robert Stephenson (1803–1859).

The locomotives were to be tried on a level stretch of railway about two miles long, and were required to make 20 return trips – about 70 miles (112 km) – at an average speed of not less than 10 m.p.h. (16 km/h). The Trials lasted several days; suffice it to say that the outstanding winner was Stephenson's *Rocket*. Note that the construction of *Rocket* was supervised by George Stephenson's son Robert (1803–1859), who was also responsible for most of the subsequent improvements.

The Liverpool and Manchester Railway opened on 15 September 1830, by which time it had eight steam locomotives. The festive occasion was marred by the first railway fatality, when Liverpool MP William Huskisson was struck down by *Rocket*. Stephenson himself drove the train carrying the dying Huskisson to Manchester at an unprecedented 36 m.p.h. (57.6 km/h).

In six months, the new railway saved Manchester manufacturers some £20,000 in transport costs. It exhibited other, less obvious, effects. From the start it carried six times as many passengers as had been expected, and after five years it was carrying half a million passengers each year. And in due course, the need for predictable timetables (in all corners of the world) would lead to standardized time, rather than the local times which had previously been perfectly adequate.

Now railways began to spread; the London to Birmingham Railway (engineer Robert Stephenson) was opened in 1837, and the following year saw the first stage of the Great Western Railway (GWR) commissioned. The engineer of the GWR was Isambard Kingdom Brunel (1806–1859), only son of Sir Marc Isambard Brunel (1769–1849). Brunel the Younger joined his father's office at the age of 17, working on the protracted Thames Tunnel of which he later became resident engineer. His outstanding works include the design for the Clifton Suspension Bridge (1829, but not finished until after his death) and the ever-larger steam-assisted sailing ships (or sail-assisted steamships) the *Great Western* (1838), the *Great Britain* (1844) and the ill-fated *Great Eastern* (1858) – and the GWR with its many fine works of civil engineering, particularly the Saltash Bridge over the River Tamar which unites Devon and Cornwall.

Brunel believed avidly in the broad-gauge railway; one whose rails are seven feet apart rather than the more usual four feet eight-and-a-half inches which

The Rainhill Trials were held in October 1829 to try and find a locomotive suitable for working the Liverpool & Manchester Railway. Mr Burstall's *Perseverance* was withdrawn from the contest at an early stage.

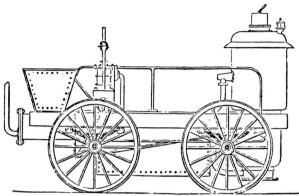

Brandreth's (or Winans') *Cycloped* was powered by a horse, and therefore disqualified. There was a suggestion that perhaps the passengers should work a treadmill to drive their own trains.

Braithwaite and Ericsson's *Novelty*. Mr Ericsson was a Swede 'who afterwards proceeded to the United States and there achieved considerable distinction as an engineer.'

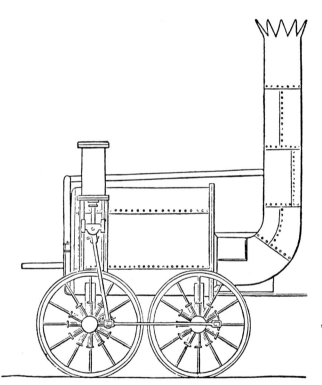

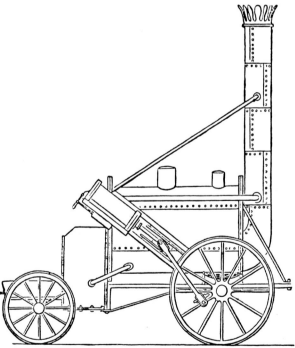

Timothy Hackworth's *Sanspareil*. Hackworth was locomotive foreman of the Stockton & Darlington Railway; no surprise that his engine is not dissimilar from *Rocket*.

The winner – R Stephenson & Co's *Rocket*, which weighed 4.25 tons and ran at an average speed of 13.8 m.p.h (22.2 km / hr), with a maximum of 29 m.p.h (46.7 km / hr).

Brunel's Great Iron Ship, the *Great Eastern*, during construction.

The *Great Eastern* ready for launching. The launch was a protracted procedure which did nothing to improve Brunel's health: he died before her maiden voyage. The *Great Eastern* was never a successful passenger boat, was turned over to laying the first transatlantic telegraph cable in 1865, and finished her days as a floating adjunct to Lewis's, the Liverpool department store.

Comparisons:
1838 the *Great Western*
1844 the *Great Britain*
1858 the *Great Eastern*

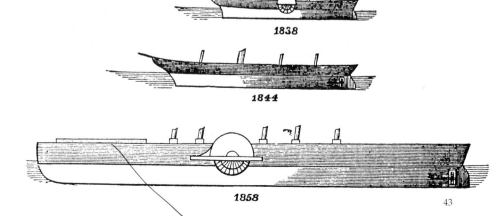

1838

1844

1858

A reception at the bottom of a shaft leading to the twin portals of the Thames Tunnel. The work began on 16 February 1825 and, after immense problems in construction, the tunnel was opened on 25 March 1843.

A sectional view of the Thames Tunnel under construction, showing Brunel's tunelling shield. Men in the shield dig out the face, the shield is jacked forward, and another ring of brickwork completed.

The Great Western Railway was converted from broad to standard gauge on 21 May 1892. Here, workers remodel the points at Plymouth. Some 5,000 men completed the conversion of 170 miles of track in 33 hours.

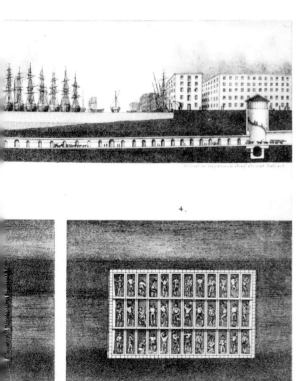

Parliament decreed to be standard in 1848. By all accounts, the broad gauge gave a wonderfully smooth ride, but that could not save it; in 1892 the GWR had 170 miles (272 km) of broad gauge and 253 miles (405 km) of mixed gauge, all reduced to the narrow standard in one great 30-hour effort (as illustrated above).

In Britain, the railways spread apace. In 1842, Queen Victoria took her first journey by train – and enjoyed it. That set the seal of approval on the enterprise. A year later, there were over 2,000 miles (3,200 km) of track. By 1844, there was so much demand for passenger travel that Parliament enacted that every railway should run at least one train – a 'Parliamentary Train' – each day with a third-class carriage offering seats at one penny per mile. 'Railway Mania' hit the country; at its height in 1846, 272 Acts of Parliament for new railways were passed.

In 1863, there were over 10,000 miles (16,000 km) of track; over 16,000 (25,600 km) in 1883 and over 19,000 (30,400 km) in 1903. The amount of employment the railways generated was immense: tens of thousands were engaged not only in building and running them, but in providing all the ancillary services which sprang up – from railway hotels to booking agencies; from suppliers of uniforms to printers of posters.

By the end of the 19th century, the railways were far more developed than even George Stephenson could have imagined – not only in Britain, but in most other parts of the world. But, as the railways had put the canals out of business, so would the roads threaten the railways, a process which began far earlier than most people think. As we have seen, road improvements began in earnest at about the same time as the railways emerged. A railway system needs the support of a road system, since it cannot serve every village and hamlet. People first became used to the idea of travel; then it became an expectation.

Almost everywhere which was to be served by rail had been reached by the end of the 19th century – by which time motorized road vehicles were becoming practical. The present conclusion is a fast, safe railway system complemented by a road system of limited safety and speed, with the canals and lesser railways taking their places more as means of leisure.

Obsolete broad gauge locomotives in the 'mortuary' at Swindon, waiting to be broken up.

Right
'The last rail is laid, the last spike driven home. The Pacific Railroad is finished.' Thus was the completion of the world's biggest railroad feat announced by telegraph from Promontory, Utah on 10 May 1869. The first sod of the new railroad had been cut at Sacramento, California on 22 February 1863; there had been a problem getting started because of an argument about the gauge, and the other end was then further delayed because of an argument between the railroad company and Abraham Lincoln about the position of the railhead. Eventually work got under way and, after overcoming untold hardships, the two construction columns met some six years later. It was astonishing that, instead of joining the rails with jubilation and festivity as expected, the building crews redoubled their efforts and passed one another, continuing to lay parallel lines for 225 miles (360 km) before the rival railroad companies started to count the cost and called a halt to the farce.

Trestle bridge across Papio Valley, Omaha, Nebraska, under construction.

Textile machinery

One of the first industries in Britain to benefit from the climate of development – and, indeed, feed it with ideas and demands – was the textile industry. It was transformed from a hearthside cottage industry to a powerful national activity, with factories based in growing towns such as Manchester, and with ports such as Liverpool developing to shift raw materials and products in and out of the country.

In 1733, John Kay (?–1764) invented the flying shuttle, an improvement to looms that enabled weavers to weave faster. The shuttle, containing a bobbin on to which the weft (the crossways yarn in weaving) yarn was wound, was normally pushed from one side of the warp (the series of yarns extended lengthways in a loom) to the other by hand. A broad-loom needed two weavers to throw the shuttle. Now the flying shuttle was thrown by a lever operated by one weaver. Despite this improvement, the invention wasn't taken up widely until the 1750s, probably because Kay didn't put much effort into spreading the word. Communications in those days were slow and a craftsman with such an invention would have enough to do supplying the local weavers. Once the use of the flying shuttle became widespread it caused a shortage

Fibres such as flax, cotton and wool tend to cling together, and so can be spun into yarn by drawing and twisting. The mass of fibre is held on a distaff; the hand spinner pulls them out and twists them, then winds them on to a drop spindle.

About the 14th century, the hand-spinning principle was transferred to the spinning wheel, worked first by hand, then by a treadle.

On the floor to the left is a pair of carding combs for teasing out the fibres before spinning.

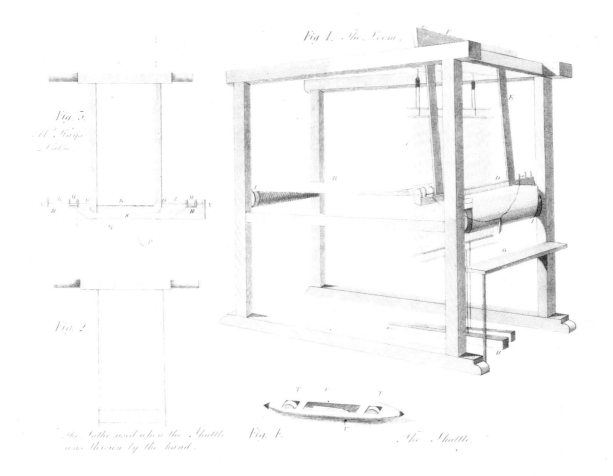

Fig 1. The Loom.

Fig 5.
Mʳ Kays
Patent.

Fig 2

Fig 3.

the Lathe used when the Shuttle
was thrown by the hand.

Fig 4.

The Shuttle.

A simple loom divides the warp threads (running in a horizontal sheet B) into two sets – all the even-numbered threads and all the odd-numbered threads. One set is pulled up and the other pulled down by means of vertical frames C worked by pedals M.

The shuttle is then passed through the gap (or 'shed'), paying out its weft thread behind it. The 'up' warp set is then pulled down, the 'down' set pulled up, and the shuttle passed back again.

This process builds up a woven cloth. John Kay invented a means of throwing a wheeled shuttle (Fig 4) back and forth by pulling a handle one way and the other (Fig 3). This enabled the shuttle to travel further, and the weaver to work faster.

The frame shown in Fig 2 is for beating against the weft to make the material more compact.

of yarn and fuelled the search for a faster method of spinning.

At that time, yarn was spun either by hand, or on the well-known traditional spinning wheel. The first machine to improve on the spinning wheel was invented by James Hargreaves (?–1788) some time in the 1760s; he named it the 'spinning jenny' after his wife. A carriage pulled away from the raw cotton, emulating the action of a hand spinner. The drawn-out thread was then wound on to a spindle as the carriage returned. The hand-powered jenny produced several threads at once and increased a spinner's output eight-fold. However, the machine did not twist the thread enough to give it sufficient strength for the warp; it was suitable only for weft – but it was a start. Unfortunately for Hargreaves, he sold models of his invention before trying to patent it, in 1769; then he found he couldn't because it was already in use.

The year that Hargreaves was unsuccessful with his

Hargreaves' spinning jenny (1764) imitates the action of the hand spinner, drawing out the fibres with a moving carriage and twisting them into yarns, which are then wound on to bobbins. Hargreaves' first jenny had eight spindles. As the number of spindles on the frame was increased the work became heavier and heavier, so jennies were installed in larger and larger workshops. Hand spinners feared that they would lose their living and in 1768 a group broke into Hargreaves' Blackburn workshop and smashed his machines. He moved to Nottingham, where his machines became widely used, despite opposition. Hargreaves applied for a patent in 1769, just after Arkwright applied for his. Hargreaves' patent was not granted, because he had sold some machines so his idea wasn't secret any more. Jenny-spun yarn was suitable for weft, but not strong enough for warp.

Richard Arkwright's 'water frame' (Patent No. 931 of 1769). The fibres are drawn, twisted, and wound on bobbins similar to those of a spinning wheel – clearly seen at the bottom of the frame. The machine was driven by a water wheel, hence the name 'water frame'. Arkwright's machine was too big and heavy to be used in the home, so he built a factory at Nottingham, producing cotton cloth using his 'water twist' for warp and jenny-spun yarn for weft. In 1771, he built another factory at Cromford in Derbyshire, where there was plenty of water power. Arkwright would nowadays be described as an 'entrepreneur', building more factories and continuing to invent machinery for them. Arkwright's factory at Shude Hill, Manchester, was set up in about 1780; it was the first to use steam as motive power but, instead of using a Watt rotative engine, he used a Newcomen engine to pump water to feed a water wheel.

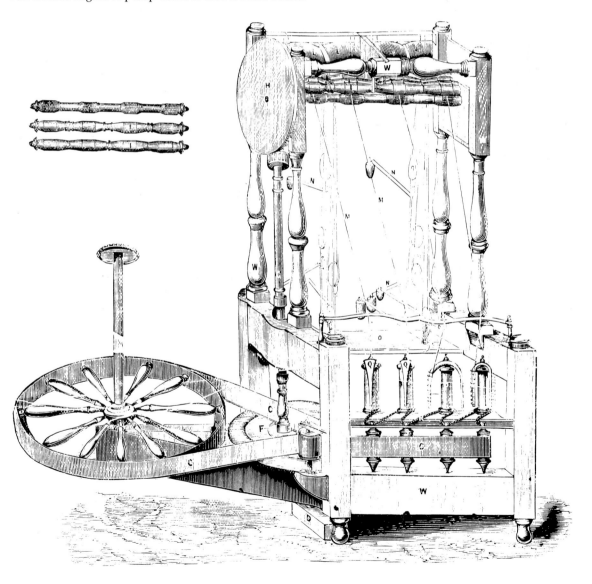

patent application, Richard Arkwright patented his spinning machine. He had intended it to be powered by a horse but the first models were powered by water wheels, so the device came to be called the water frame. This spinning machine gave the thread a twist as it was pulled through two sets of rollers; this made it strong enough to be used for both weft and warp. The water frame was the first powered textile machine, and marked the move away from traditional domestic manufacture, toward factory production where one power source could drive many machines.

In 1779 Samuel Crompton (1753–1827) produced his spinning mule. This device combined the moving carriage of the spinning jenny with the rollers of the water frame, and gave the spinner great control over the process, making it suitable for spinning many different types of yarn. Although the water frame had been powered, Crompton's mule was hand driven, which shows that, at that time, the use of power to drive machinery was by no means a foregone conclusion. Not only were the machines complex, taking longer to develop; there was still no rotary drive from the steam engine for those without a suitable mill-stream avail-

Samuel Crompton's spinning mule of 1779 combined features of Hargreaves' jenny and Arkwright's water frame. The mule was developed to spin many threads at one time as is seen in this early 19th century view of a powered mule-spinning shed. The mule on the left has just wound its carriage in; the carriage of the mule on the right has reached the end of its outward travel. Note the sweeper on the floor with a hand brush – no wonder industrial accidents were common.

able. Powered machines had to be turned by water wheels and, if there was no stream, water had to be pumped by a steam engine.

As the flying shuttle had produced a demand for yarn, so the spinning jenny, water frame and mule satisfied that demand and more, creating a demand for some means of using the excess yarn. That something was, of course, a faster loom. It is reasonable to assume that people were trying to develop powered looms even before there was an excess of yarn. However, some of the problems of getting such a complex machine to operate under power must have seemed

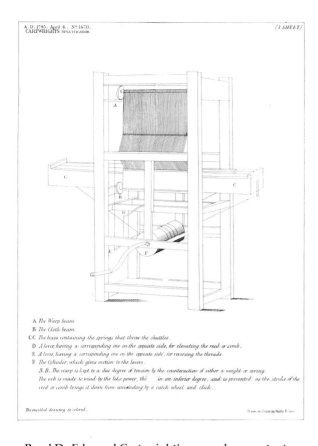

A.D. 1785. April 4. Nº 1470.
CARTWRIGHTS SPECIFICATION.
(1 SHEET)

A The Warp beam.
B The Cloth beam.
CC The boxes containing the springs that throw the shuttles.
D A lever, having a corresponding one on the opposite side, for elevating the reed, or comb.
E A lever, having a corresponding one on the opposite side, for reversing the threads.
F The Cylinder, which gives motion to the levers.
N.B. The warp is kept to a due degree of tension by the counteraction of either a weight or spring.
The web is made to wind by the like power, tho' in an inferior degree, and is prevented as the stroke of the
reed or comb brings it down from unwinding by a ratch wheel and click.

The enabled drawing is colored.

Drawn on Stone by Malby & Sons

Revd Dr Edmund Cartwright's power loom patent 1470 of 1785. Cartwright was on holiday in Derbyshire when he heard a spinner say that there was now so much yarn that hands would never be found to weave it. 'To this I replied', wrote Cartwright, 'that Arkwright must set his wits to work and invent a weaving mill.' The spinners said this was impossible, so Cartwright set to work to prove them wrong. His first power loom needed two strong men to work it. Watt's steam engine was the answer, and he bought one to drive his improved looms. But while others benefited from his invention, Cartwright became more and more in debt and had to give up his mills at Doncaster in 1793. In 1809, Parliament recognized his contribution to the prosperity of the country and awarded him £10,000, which enabled him to retire to a small farm.

pretty insurmountable at a time when there was little tradition of loom design. Ways had to be found of translating the power from whatever source into the various movements that a loom demanded. Moreover, the machine had to stop if a yarn broke, to prevent it producing an ineluctable jumble of knots. In 1784, Edmund Cartwright (1743–1823) produced his first attempt at a powered loom; though it didn't work, it showed him the way, and the following year he patented a power loom which did work. Even so, the technology of the time was scarcely adequate, and Cartwright's loom was not really a practical proposition. The one thing it did do was to show inventors that such mechanization was possible. However, powered looms were not sufficiently well developed to be widely used until the second decade of the 19th century.

In the United States, the textile industry was slower to get started. When the merchants of New England started to invest in cotton mills at the end of the 18th century, they sent half a dozen people to Britain to recruit skilled labour. The result was that a law was passed in England forbidding the export of textile machinery and the textile 'brain drain'. However, in a feat of industrial espionage Samuel Slater (1768–1835), the superintendent of a Lancashire mill, memorized the plans and surreptitiously crossed the Atlantic. He set up mills at Rhode Island and Massachusetts, becoming one of America's leading manufacturers.

In 1825, Parliament repealed the ban, and from then on many British textile workers were encouraged by American employers to emigrate with their machines and help to establish and expand the industry in the United States. It was at about this time that Lowell, MA was established by a group of Boston merchants. 25 miles (40 km) north of Boston, the Merrimac River falls some 33 feet (10 m), and was able to provide water power for a number of textile factories. By 1860, Lowell had 12,000 looms and a population approaching 40,000. The success of the 'Lowell System' gave rise to a number of similar towns along the Merrimac, and into Southern Maine.

An early 19th-century powered weaving shed – each girl attends two looms.

Huge factories were established within a few decades of the invention of spinning and weaving equipment. Messrs Swainson, Birley & Co's factory near Preston in Lancashire was seven storeys high, 158 yards (144.5 m) long and 18 yards (16.5 m) broad. Its 660 windows held 32,500 panes of glass.

Industrial chemistry

At the beginning of the Industrial Revolution, chemistry was far from the systematic study we know today. In 1740, only 13 of the substances we now call elements were known. The list included metals such as copper, lead, tin, silver, gold and mercury, which had been around for thousands of years. The alchemists of old recognized four 'elements' – air, earth, fire and water. They had applied much intellect to the search for the Philosopher's Stone, which would transmute base metals into gold. But by the 18th century, it was clear that there must be an underlying pattern to chemistry as there was to everything else, and alchemical magic turned to science in 1757 when Professor Joseph Black of Glasgow (James Watt's mentor) identified carbon dioxide (CO_2). Cavendish discovered hydrogen in 1766, and Scheele and Priestley (independently) discovered oxygen in about 1772.

Lavoisier (1743–1794) demonstrated that oxygen was a component of air, thus destroying two myths at once – that phlogiston was the supposed 'fiery principle' within flammable matter which supported combustion, and that air was one of the 'elements'. Cavendish discovered that hydrogen and oxygen combined to make water, and Lavoisier succeeded in generating hydrogen by passing steam over red-hot iron, thus removing another of the alchemists' 'elements' from the list.

By now the idea of elements being substances incapable of being decomposed further, first proposed by Robert Boyle (1627–1691), had taken hold. Chemistry really took off towards the end of the 18th century, and the beginning of the 19th: 19 further elements were identified between 1740 and 1800, and a further 51 during the 19th century.

At the same time, an understanding of the way elements combined developed, as did techniques for

Joseph Priestley (1733–1804), one of the pioneers of chemistry, whose attacks on the established church led to his being hounded to the United States in 1794. *Right below* **The mob burning Priestley's house at Birmingham, England: a demonstration against his religious views.**

Antoine Laurent Lavoisier (1743–1794), who published his first paper on chemistry at the age of 22. His career was curtailed by the guillotine during the French Revolution.

Sir Humphry Davy (1778–1829) – who discovered more elements than anyone else.

Of all the people who figured in this period, few contributed more than Michael Faraday (1791–1867). Apart from his demonstration of the relationship between magnetism and electricity in 1831, which laid the foundation for the dynamo and the electric motor, and his studies of electroplating, he made many other discoveries in many fields of science.

manufacturing chemical compunds. In 1800, the Italian physicist Alessandro Volta (1745–1827) announced the invention of his 'voltaic pile' or electric battery. Seven years later Humphry Davy (1778–1829) discovered the elemental metals potassium and sodium by passing electric currents through caustic potash and caustic soda.

In 1828, Friedrich Wöhler (1800–1890) synthesized urea from ammonium cyanate, establishing a connection between what came to called organic and inorganic chemistry. The importance of this new branch of chemistry grew apace; it now embraces diverse fields such as fuels, explosives, synthetic fibres, dyes, perfumes, pharmaceuticals and plastics. Coal tar – the 'exceedingly complex' mixture of materials which is released when coal is heated to make coke and coal gas – was found to be rich in organic substances, and itself formed a foundation for a new industry.

The improvement in chemical knowledge and techniques had an effect on almost every part of the industrial revolution. As more and more chemical elements, and the ways in which they combined, were discovered, chemistry turned from an art to a science, preparation techniques for useful industrial chemicals were developed, and the knowledge of what those chemicals did improved. For example, alkalis for glass-makers, soap-makers and bleachers began to be synthesized at the end of the 18th century, as plant ash which they traditionally used was in shorter supply.

One way to judge the level of a country's industrialization is to measure its use of sulphuric acid. Sulphuric acid was used to extract metals, to bleach textiles, and later to produce chlorine to do the same job. Dyers used it to dissolve indigo; later it was used to make soda and a range of other salts, including phosphates for agricultural fertilizers.

Agriculture

In medieval times, a large proportion of the working population worked on the land. The work was labour intensive, the only non-human power employed being oxen to pull ploughs and horses to turn butter-churning equipment and the like. On a typical farm of the period, many men would work on ploughing a large field, which was divided up into long, thin strips as ploughing progressed. These strips were allocated in turn to the farmers, who sowed their crops as they went. By the end of the season each man would typically have several acres of corn, but laid down in many strips.

Like everything else, farming practice was ripe for a change. Long-term, there were three main effects. Firstly, advances in science brought new knowledge about how plants grow and what chemicals to put on the land to improve crop yields. Secondly, there were developments in basic tools such as ploughs and harrows, and more advanced machines such as reapers and threshers, made possible by improved materials and techniques. Thirdly, the increasing mechanization in farming, and the growing demand for labour from manufacturing industries, resulted in a shift of population from country to town.

An early advance was the seed drill, the best known of which is Jethro Tull's of 1701. Educated at Eton and Oxford, Tull inherited a farm at Basildon in Berkshire

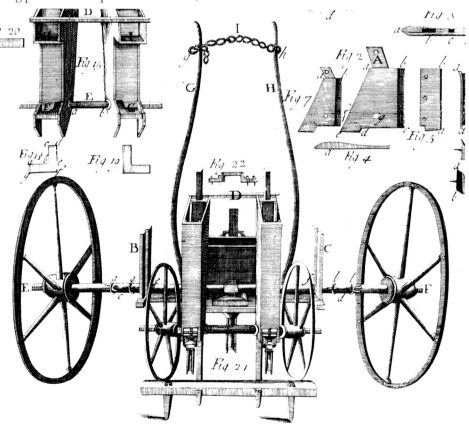

Jethro Tull (1674–1741) saw the advantage of sowing seed sparingly in rows, rather than scattering it all over the land. The ground is then harrowed to cover the seed. This is Tull's diagram of his seed 'drill'.

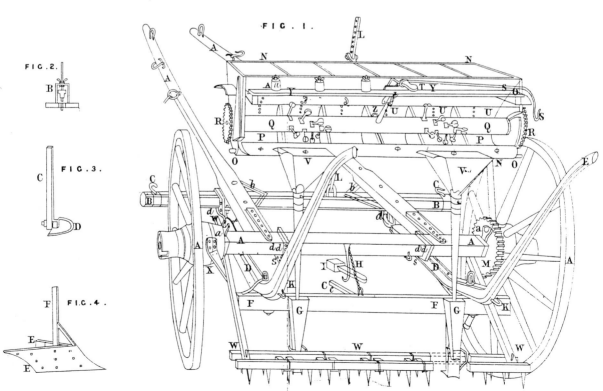

FIG. 1.

FIG. 2.

FIG. 3.

FIG. 4.

Left above
Left above
Wright's seed drill (Patent No. 1014 of 1787). Apart from forming the furrow in which the seeds are planted, the other function of the drill is to mete out the seed. The gears driving the measuring mechanism are seen behind the main wheel of the drill.

Left below
James Cooke's seed drill (Patent No. 1659 of 1788), the forerunner of the modern drill. This drawing shows a seed-measuring mechanism more clearly. The little spoons on the shaft QQ pick up set amounts of seed and drop them into funnels which are set above the furrows made by members shown in Fig 4. The mechanism is shown raised up for clarity; in practice, the gear wheels M on the main wheels drive gear wheels R on the seed-box, which would be mounted below the main shaft AA.

Below
Patrick Bell's reaper (1826). As with all reapers, the rotating sails push the stalks of the crop against the shearing teeth of a cutter-bar.

and began to use it as a vehicle for his inventiveness. He found that seed grew better when planted at a given depth and spacing than when it was scattered in the traditional way. His drill enabled him to obtain twice the yield from a third of the seed from a given piece of land. Moreover, seeds germinating in rows were easier to hoe, and Tull invented a horse hoe to facilitate this back-breaking work. In spite of his success, Tull's methods were scarcely exploited and developed before his death in 1741.

Tull was not alone in his experiments; indeed, the landowners of the time led developments in agriculture and husbandry. Although many contributed, one of the best publicized was Lord Townshend (1674–1738; 'Turnip' Townshend) of Norfolk, who devised a four-year crop-rotation system – clover, wheat, turnips, barley – obviating the need to let land lie fallow every third year. Townshend also invented 'marling' – digging up the lower clay and mixing it with topsoil.

The widespread introduction of turnips provided animal feed for the winter, so herds no longer had to be slaughtered wholesale in the autumn. An understanding of breeding animals dawned, pioneered by people such as Robert Bakewell (1725–1795) of Dishley in Leicestershire.

The benign interest of landowners such as Coke of Holkham (1752–1842) and the Dukes of Bedford was reflected in their annual displays of livestock, crops and machinery which attracted visitors from all over the country and laid the foundation of the present-day

Cyrus McCormick's American reaping machine (1831). In Bell's reaper (page 59) the horses push so as to avoid trampling the uncut crop. McCormick's reaper has a shaft at one side so that the horses walk on an already-cut path.

agricultural show.

The most labour-intensive task on the farm was harvesting, and reaping and threshing machines would generate much interest. Patrick Bell of Forfarshire built a successful reaping machine in 1826; in America, Cyrus McCormick produced his reaper in 1831 when he was only 22 years of age. A later development was to bind the corn as it was cut. Threshing was traditionally carried out with flails, and early machines – such as Menzies' water-powered patent of 1737 – sought to emulate the flailing action. In fact, a rubbing action proved better, and the first successful machine on such a principle was built by Andrew Meikle of East Lothian in 1786 – to be driven by human, horse or water power. The modern threshing machine was born when Meikle's principle was combined with a winnowing fan (to blow away the chaff) and grading screens – which took another half century or so. Portable threshing machines, driven by the power take-off on a traction engine, became the norm until the development of the combine harvester which performs all the actions, leaving bales of straw behind and discharging its grain periodically into a trailer pulled by

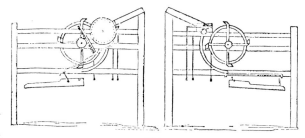

Fig. I
1786. First form of Meikle's Thrashing Machine

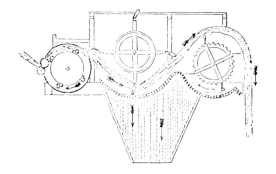

Andrew Meikle's first threshing machine (1786). A rotating member carries arms which imitate the action of hand flails. Grain drops out through the bottom, and straw is carried out to the right of the machine.

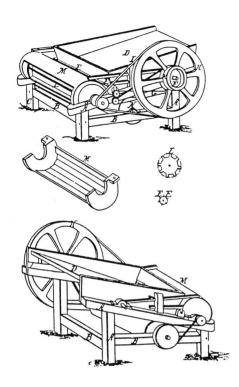

a tractor moving beside it.

Agriculture in Britain was on a somewhat domestic scale, compared with that in the United States, where there was a vast amount of land and a relatively small population. Once established, the inventive skill of the pioneers again came to the fore. Apart from the highly-succesful McCormick's reaper, most machinery development before 1850 was carried out in Britain; after that date, American developments became more important.

In that sense, agricultural developments sum up the period of the industrial revolution. The equipment which was in use in 1850 was the result of a century and a half of intense change. Once it had reached that point, much of it was to remain the same for many decades to come.

Left
Slater's thrashing – or threshing – machine: an American patent of 1830.

Once a common sight – a traction engine driving a threshing machine. This scene was drawn in about 1850, but was not unknown a century later.

Fowler's improved compound self-moving ploughing engine (about 1865). The cable which pulls the plough across the field is wound on a drum beneath the engine. The engine then moves forward a little, and the plough is reversed and pulled back. Either the engines were used in pairs, one on either side of the field, or a pulley was anchored on the other side so that one engine could pull the plough in either direction.

Grafton's locomotive cultivator, 1860. This machine is for 'harrowing, drilling, hoeing, harvesting and carting entirely by means of steam.' The implements are carried across the field on the 50 foot (15 m) booms, which are mounted on caterpillar tracks of very strong indiarubber reinforced with linen threads and shod with iron on wooden baulks. When the machine has finished its work it is run on to a traverse, the tracks mounted on rails seen in the foreground, and moved sideways for its next run.

Chronology

1701	Tull's seed drill		1792	Trevithick's engine
1702	Savery's 'miner's friend'		1801	Trevithick's steam carriage
1709	Iron smelted by coke		1802	*Charlotte Dundas*
1712	Newcomen's engine		1804	Trevithick's steam locomotive
1733	Kay's flying shuttle		1807	Mechanical mine ventilation
1740	Blister steel			*Clermont*
1745	Lee's windmill		1808	*Catch-me-who-can*
1754	First steam engine in US		1813	*Puffing Billy*
1761	Duke of Bridgewater's canal		1815	Miner's safety lamp
1764	Watt's experiments		1819	McAdam's roads
	Hargreaves' spinning jenny		1825	Stockton & Darlington railway
1769	Watt's improved engine		1826	Bell's reaper
	Arkwright's water frame		1828	Nielson's hot blast furnace
1775	Watt's double-acting engine			Wöhler's synthesis of urea
1777	The first iron bridge		1830	Liverpool & Manchester railway
1779	Crompton's spinning mule			Trevithick's rock drill
1784	Watt's parallel motion		1831	McCormick's reaper
	Cort's puddled iron		1839	Naysmith's steam hammer
1785	Steam-driven factory		1843	Thames tunnel opened
	Cartwright's power loom		1858	Brunel's *Great Eastern*
1786	Meikle's threshing machine		1860	Bessemer's steel-making process

Further reading

Isaac Asimov
Asimov's Chronology of Science and Discovery
New York, Harper Collins 1989

Asa Briggs
Iron Bridge to Crystal Palace
New York, Thames & Hudson 1979

David F Hawke
Nuts & Bolts of the Past: A History of American Technology
New York, HarperCollins 1989

Brooke Hindle & Stephen Lubar
Engines of Change: The American Industrial Revolution 1790–1860
Washington DC, Smithsonian 1986

Ann L Macdonald
Feminine Ingenuity: Women and Invention in America
New York, Ballantine 1992

Peter North
The Wall Chart of Discovery and Inventon
London, Studio Editions Ltd 1991

LTC Rolt
Victorian Engineering
London, Penguin 1988

Robert Routledge
Discoveries and Inventions of the Nineteenth Century
(reprint) London, Bracken 1989

Charles Singer, EJ Holmyard *et al*
A History of Technology
Oxford 1958

Samuel Smiles
The Lives of the Engineers (3 vols)
London, Murray 1860;
Newton Abbot, David & Charles reprint 1968 ;
Selections MIT 1966

Samuel Smiles
Industrial Biography
London, Murray 1883;
Newton Abbot, David & Charles 1967

Victorian Inventions
John Murray/Trafalgar Square 1992

Christine Vialls
The Industrial Revolution Begins
Minneapolis, Lerner 1982

David Weitzmann
Windmills, Bridges and Old Machines: Discovering our Industrial Past
New York, Macmillan 1982

Trevor I Williams
The History of Inventions from Stone Axes to Silicon Chips
New York, Facts on File 1987

Index

Animal power 6
Arkwright, Richard 50
Bakewell, Robert 59
Barton Aqueduct 30
Bedford, Dukes of 59
Bell, Patrick 58, 60
Bessemer, Henry 19, 21
Bingley Locks 32
Black, Dr Joseph 11, 55
Blackett, Mr 37
Blacksmith 21
Blast furnace 17
Blenkinsop, Mr 37
Blister steel 17
Boroughbridge 27
Bough, Robert 55
Boulton & Watt 12, 14
Boulton, Matthew 6, 11
Boyle, Robert 55
Braithwaite & Ericsson 40, 42
Brandreth, Mr 40, 42
Bridgewater canal 28
    Duke of 28, 34, 39
Brindley, James 28
Broad gauge 41, 45, 46
Brunel, Isambard Kingdom 41,
    43
    Sir Marc Isambard 41
Burleigh's rock drill 25
Burstall, Mr 40, 42
Caledonian Canal 32
Calley, John 8
Canal mania 31
Carnegie, Andrew 21
Cartwright, Edmund 53
Catch-me-who-can 36
Chat Moss 39
Charlotte Dundas 34
Clermont 34
Clifton Suspension Bridge 41
Coal 4
    gas 17
    tar 17, 56
Coalbrookdale 15
Coke 17
    of Holkham 59
Connections 4
Cook's Kitchen Mine 15
Cooke's seed drill 58
Cornish engine 15
Cornwall 12, 14, 17, 31
Cort, Henry 19
Cromford 51
Crompton, Samuel 52
Culross Abbey 17

Cycloped 40, 42
Darby, Abraham I 17; II 19
Davy, Sir Humphry 25, 56
Ding Dong Mine 15
Dudley Castle 9
Dundas, Lord 32
Dundonald, Lord 17
Ellesmere Canal 31
Erie Canal 32
Experiment 38, 39
Faraday, Michael 56
'Fire man' 24
Forge hammer 23
Fowler's ploughing engine 62
Fuel, shortage of 17
Fulton, Robert 34, 35
Geordie lamp 25
Gilbert, John 28
Glasgow 11
Grafton's locomotive
    cultivator 62
Grasshopper engine 16
Great Britain 41, 44
Great Eastern 41, 44
Great Western 41, 44
Great Western Railway 41, 45
Hackworth, Timothy 40, 42
Hale, Stephen 17
Hargreaves, James 49, 50
Harrogate 26
Hebburn colliery 24
Holyhead 27
Hot-blast furnace 23
Hudson River 32, 34
Huntsman, Benjamin 17
Huskisson, William 41
Industrial revolution defined 5
Ironbridge 20
Iron smelting 4
Kay, John 48
Knaresborough, Blind Jack of
    see Metcalf, John
Killingworth 37
Lavoisier, Antoine 55
Lee's wind mill 5
Lincoln, Abraham 46
Liverpool 32, 35, 48
Liverpool – Manchester Canal
    35, 36
Llangollen Canal 31
Locomotive 37
Loom 48, 49, 54
Lowell, MA 53
Mackworth, Sir Humphrey 36
Man engine 24

Manchester 28, 30, 32, 35, 41, 48
McAdam, John Loudon 27
McCormick, Cyrus 60
Meikle, Andrew 60
Menai Straits Bridge 27
Mersey 28
Metcalf, John 26
Miller, Patrick 42
Mills 5
Miner's Friend 8
Miner's safety lamp 25
Miners 6, 24
Mine ventilation 24
Mule spinning 52
Murdock, William 12, 14, 36
Naysmith, James 22, 23
Neilson, James Beaumont 23
Neptune's staircase 32
New York 32, 36
New York City 16
Newcomen, Thomas 8, 51
    engine 16
Novelty 40, 42
Pacific Railroad 46, 47
Papio Valley 47
Papplewick 14
Parliamentary Trains 43
Pease, Edward 37
Pen-y-Darren 15
Peninsular War 21
Pennsylvania 21, 34
Perserverance 40, 42
Philosopher's Stone 55
Pig iron 18
Ploughing engine 62
Plunger-pole engine 16
Pont Cysyllte 31
Potter, Humphrey 9
Priestley, Joseph 55
Providence, RI 16
Puddling 19
Puffing Billy 37
Queen Victoria 43
Railway 38
Railway mania 43
Rainhill Trials 40, 42
Rennie, John 31
Reverbatory furnace 19
River Dee 31, 32
Rocket 40
Roebuck, Dr John 11
Saltash Bridge 41
Sandars, Mr 37
Savery, Thomas 8
Schuyler Mine 16

Seed drills 57
Sisson, Jonathan 11
Slater, Samuel 53
Smeaton, John 9, 10
Soho Works 12, 14
Spinning 48
    jenny 49, 52
    wheel 48
Stafford, Marquess of 40
Staffordshire 31
Steam hammer 22, 23
Steel 17
Stephenson, George 25, 37, 40,
    45
    Robert 27, 41
Stevens, John & Robert 34
Stockton & Darlington railway
    37, 42
Struvé's ventilator 24
Strip farming 57
Sulphuric acid 56
Swainson, Birley & Co 54
Symington, William 32, 34
Telford, Thomas 26, 32
Threshing machine 60
Townshend, Lord 'Turnip' 59
Traction engine 61
Trestle Bridge 47
Trevithick, Richard 25, 36, 37
Tull, Jethro 57, 58
Tunnels: Hoosac, Mont Cenis,
    Simplon 25; Thames 41, 43
Turnpike Trusts 26
Volta, Alessandro 56
Water frame 51, 52
Watt, James 10, 19, 51, 53
    single-acting engine 11
    double-acting engine 12, 14
    crank designs 13
    parallel motion 14
    governor 14
Wedgwood, Josiah 30
Wheal Treasury Mine 15
White Horse Tavern 29
Wilkinson, John 'Iron Mad' 19
Winans, Mr 40, 42
Wöhler, Friedrick 56
Worsley 28
Wright's seed drill 58
Wylam Colliery 37
Wylam Dilly 37

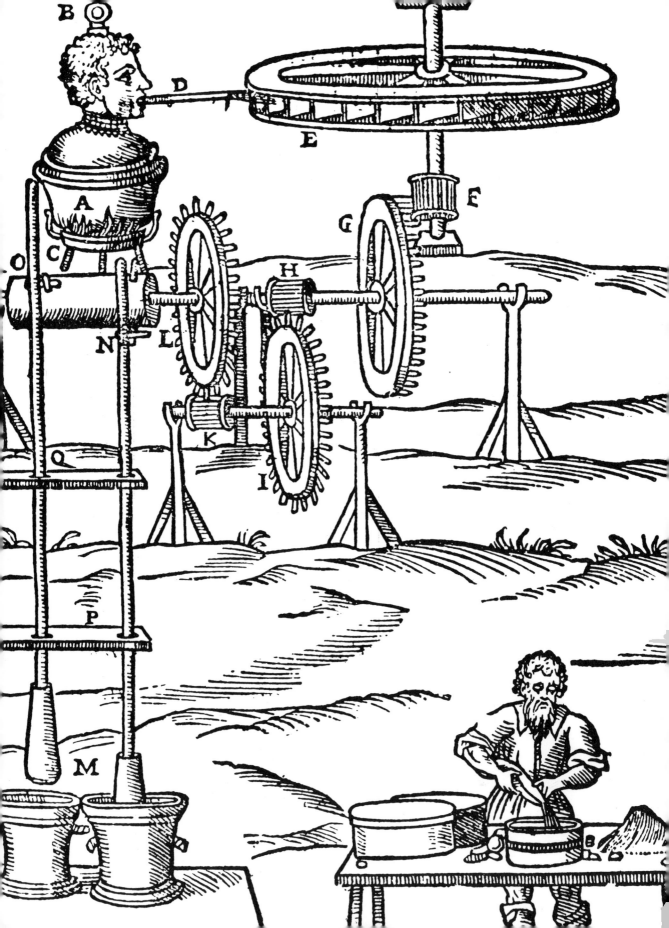